Dreamland park c1922

Dreamland Revived

The story of Margate's famous amusement park
by NICK EVANS

Bygone Publishing

A catalogue record for this book is available from the British Library.

ISBN 978-0-9566172-2-4

First published in 2003 as Dreamland Remembered.

Printed and bound in Northern Ireland by W&G Baird, Antrim.

Front cover photographs:
Top, Margate seafront, 1963, by unknown photographer
Bottom, Dreamland park at night, 1965, Elmar Ludwig © John Hinde Archive.

Back cover photograph:
Dreamland park, (Bemboms) c1982, by unknown photographer.

Contents

Introduction   4

First awakenings   (1863-1919)   5

Making the dream
come true   (1920-1945)   11

Post war revival   (1946-1969)   51

New brooms herald
a new era   (1970-1981)   82

The Bembom years   (1982-1995)   97

To the Millennium
– and beyond   (1996-2009)   105

Building a new dream   (2010-2014)   120

Acknowledgements   128

Introduction

Ever since Dreamland's closure was first mooted in 2003 hardly a month has gone by without the park, its rides or the cinema catching the attention of local, and sometimes national, media. What happens to Dreamland is an ongoing story and I share the hopes of many that its reopening will be the new beginning everyone so keenly wishes to see.

The journey has as many highs and lows as the park's wonderful Scenic Railway. The listed structure has dominated the place for the best part of a century and, despite the damaging fire of April 2008, has become a symbol of hope in the quest to regenerate Dreamland – and ultimately Margate itself.

I have long said that youth was never properly misspent without visiting the park at least a couple of times in adolescence. Many have fond memories of the Scenic Railway as well as the Big Wheel, the Caterpillar the Looping Star, the River Caves and the lines of sideshows.

An outing to Margate simply wasn't complete without a walk around Dreamland – indeed it was often the main reason for going to the east Kent resort every summer. As a result, the two became synonymous with one another.

Dreamland was designed to appeal across the age range but there was more than just the amusement park to enjoy. Cinemas, ballroom dancing, discos, bingo, summer shows, skating – ice and roller – and squash have all been part of the seafront scene over the years. This book looks at Dreamland from its beginnings, its heydays immediately before and after World War Two as well as its fall from favour as society's expectations of leisure and holiday time changed. It also brings light to the ideas and plans finally taking shape in the park for the 2015 reopening.

Many of the photographs in this book formed the holding company's own publicity material handed on to my late father Bill Evans, who was Dreamland's press officer from the early 1970s until the Bembom Brothers took over in 1981. Much of the history was also collected by Bill throughout this period. Without his careful stewardship of this material, one can only guess at what might have otherwise happened to it.

Other photographs and information have been kindly supplied by several people including Messrs Raymond Dolling, Anthony Lee, John Nurden, Bob Prett, Joe Studt and John T Williams – I am indebted to all of them. A full list of acknowledgements can be found on the last page of this book.

It is also right to give credit to the photographers hired by Margate Estates Ltd, Dreamland's holding company for 50 years, who captured the classic images in the first place, among them Edward Cox and Sunbeam Photos, as well as the Isle of Thanet Gazette.

Days at Dreamland evoke nostalgic memories for many people and I hope they flood back with this book as the park prepares for its long overdue revival.

Nick Evans
Whitstable
May 2014

1. *This is the earliest known view of Spiers & Pond's Hall By The Sea which can be seen on the right and would have been taken during the late 1860s. The man standing fourth from left was known as the Margate Strongman and he was hanged after raping and killing a young woman in the gardens in 1895.*

First awakenings

Dreamland's origins can be traced back to 1863 when rival railway companies found themselves at loggerheads bringing trippers to Margate, a lucrative trade, for the town had become a fast growing seaside resort.

The South Eastern Railway had opened its line to the town in 1846 from Ramsgate but now arch rival London, Chatham & Dover Railway was trying to muscle in on the act and break SER's monopoly.

Confident of winning parliamentary permission, LCDR built a terminus on the seafront right next door to SER's station, and even ran a test train there in May 1864. But the move meant the rival's sets of tracks were interwoven and so the railway inspectorate refused to sanction the new development.

Undaunted, LCDR decided to build another station a short distance away calling it Margate West to serve passengers from London and Medway. Initially intended as a terminus, the company was given permission to continue the line to Ramsgate before the track was laid so plans were revised to make it a through station.

All this expensive railway wrangling saw a new building standing empty until 1867 when LCDR finally solved the problem by leasing it to its catering contractor Spiers & Pond.

The caterers christened the building The Hall By The Sea, opening it as a dance hall to satisfy the latest crazes of the lancers, the quadrille and the polka. Some 2,000 people could sashay to their heart's delight in what was one of the largest ballrooms in the country.

The manager, EP Hingston, and his successor Edward Murray, presented a variety of entertainments. Operatic and orchestral concerts were held and there were continual balls and dances, notably the annual Regatta Ball and fundraising nights for the Margate Surf Boat (predecessor of the lifeboat).

Inside, drapes were hung from the ceilings and walls, barely disguising its origins as a railway station. Despite these efforts, The Hall By The Sea was considered inferior to the long established and well-appointed Assembly Rooms in Cecil Square whose ideas it copied.

The Hall proved to be one of Spiers & Pond's less successful ventures – the company was better known as a pioneer of station buffets and refreshment cars – and by 1870 the decision was taken to pull out.

By now the passing of the Bank Holiday Act and Gladstone's 'Penny per Mile' rail legislation had started to see the lower middle and working classes coming in great numbers to the seaside. They wanted something more down-to-earth – dancing was not for them. The building was put up for auction but failed to find a buyer. Later though it was sold privately to Alderman Thomas Dalby Reeve, then Mayor of Margate, and a prosperous local businessman.

He paid £3,750 for the Hall, along with a non-commissioned railway embankment running from it, and nearby allotments. He went on to add a strip of land carrying a stream to Margate Harbour, known as the Dyke as well as adjoining swampland. Bordered by houses and the railway line, this area of some 20 acres was prone to flooding, ruling out use for housing.

In 1873 Reeve's son Arthur, married Harriett Sanger, daughter of the great Victorian showman 'Lord' George Sanger. The couple had met when Sanger's circus, flooded off its pitch in Margate, had been directed on to comparatively drier ground owned by the Alderman. Reeve, turning down Sanger's offer of recompense, accepted instead an invitation for his family to visit the circus and returned the hospitality by entertaining Sanger and family to tea.

At the same time as Arthur and Harriet were getting married, their fathers agreed to jointly develop The Hall By The Sea.

It should be said here that 'Lord' George Sanger was never a peer of the realm. He adopted his title because a rival, the American 'Buffalo Bill' Cody had been referred to in a court case Sanger lost as 'The Honourable William Cody'. Sanger is said by his grandson to have exclaimed: "The Honourable William Cody! If that Yankee can be an Honourable, then I shall be a ruddy Lord!" The paint pot came out right away and 'Lord' prefixed his publicity posters and wagons.

Straight away he understood what would appeal to Margate's visitors and quickly made a success of the Hall. He took over in February 1874 and this was followed by a grand opening on 27 June. The building was refurbished, becoming a restaurant by day and a ballroom at night, under the management of Arthur Reeve.

Music hall performers were brought down from London and a lively mood was ensured by the huge bar – open throughout the day and unfettered by licensing laws.

The old railway building was eventually replaced with a purpose built structure designed by Richard Dalby-Reeve, architect brother of Arthur, and opened in July 1898. It was a long narrow single-storied building with a seating capacity of 1,400 for the music hall concerts held afternoon and evening throughout the summer, after which the chairs were cleared to

2. 'Lord' George Sanger transformed the frontage of The Hall By The Sea to depict paintings of his menagerie animals and other attractions as this view of 1876 shows.

accommodate up to 3,000 for the dances ending the day's programme.

Sanger's imagination was at its best with his development of the land at the rear into a picturesque ornamental garden. The entrance, at the bottom of a slope beside the Hall, was an arched gateway in a perimeter wall made of flints and brick rubble from where paths led past shrubberies and rockeries to an imposing folly – a medieval ruined abbey – used as a bandstand with music played several times each day.

There were fishponds with fountains, a small lake fed from the Dyke, populated with waterfowl, and summerhouses offering shelter from the sun or rain. Cockatoos and macaws flew around quite freely.

The bordering embankment was decorated with plaster replicas of classical statuary painted to resemble marble – some said to be based on those in the papal Vatican City – while Sanger's less famous brother William, ran his own waxworks beside an array of swings, archery ranges, a coconut shy and a steam powered roundabout.

Furthest from the seafront was built the greatest attraction of all, an indoor menagerie with 23 cages for lions, tigers, leopards, bears, baboons and wolves. Some of the cages were extremely cramped and would shock modern day animal lovers. It must not be forgotten that for Victorians to see a wild animal in the flesh was both dangerous and exciting.

Away from the public gaze was a covered slaughter yard which despatched injured and worn-out horses from a wide area to be fed to the menagerie's residents.

A supply of fresh milk was guaranteed for The Hall By The Sea as cows grazed on lush marshy meadows beyond the gardens. Residents with jugs would queue outside the cowshed at milking time.

Thomas Dalby-Reeve died in April 1875 and Sanger purchased the freehold of the site, increasingly taking the part of prominent Margate citizen. He bought clothing and coal for the 'deserving poor' and presided at the subsequent distribution ceremonies in the Hall with the Mayor, the local vicar and others.

In April 1893, to cater for another great craze, a roller skating rink was opened at the Hall with an 8,000 square foot ivory maple floor. Daily demonstrations were given by Professor Chambers 'the skaterial king' who also provided 'instructions to ladies and gentlemen in ease and comfort and without the slightest chance of falling'.

LORD GEORGE
SANGER'S
HALL BY THE SEA
MARGATE,
ADJOINING THE TWO RAILWAY STATIONS.
ALL TRAMS STOP AT THE ENTRANCE.

Open all the Year Round

WITH VARIOUS ENTERTAINMENTS:
VARIETY CONCERTS,
PICTURES,
DANCING, SKATING, FÊTES, CARNIVALS,
GALAS AND LARGE PARTIES.
FOOTBALL, CRICKET, AND SPORTING CLUBS GROUNDS.
THE LARGEST AND GRANDEST BALLROOM IN EUROPE.

The Beautiful Old Gardens Illuminated at Night.

BILLIARD SALOON—2 GRAND TABLES,
PUBLIC AND PRIVATE BARS, SPECIAL SALOONS,
and every convenience.
FULLY LICENSED and being **FREE** all Refreshments are of
Superior Quality and at Popular Prices.

ACCOMMODATION FOR THOUSANDS!
AMUSEMENTS FOR ALL!
A HAPPY AND SAFE RESORT FOR CHILDREN!
THERE IS ONLY ONE **HALL** BY THE **SEA**
WHICH IS KNOWN ALL OVER THE WORLD!
All under the personal superveilance of
Mr. & Mrs. ARTHUR REEVE.

3. Dating from 1913, this is an advertisement from a penny programme sold at the Hall By The Sea – still referred to as Sanger's, although now owned by the Reeves.

4. Some of the Hall's lions who were captured for the camera around 1913.

Access to the gardens from the ballroom was through a tunnel built under the rink, one side of which was lined with ferns, the other an aquarium and aviary. It was in this tunnel in 1895 that a fellow known as the Margate Strongman raped and strangled a young woman. Her screams were drowned by the cries of the animals and birds disturbed by a firework display at the time. Her body was later found in the gardens.

The strongman was discovered and later hanged but is immortalised in the 1860s view of The Hall By The Sea as one of the seafront bystanders – see page five. The ghost was said to haunt that part of Dreamland. A medium visiting the site in the 1990s said the spirit was disturbed at being described as a prostitute and since that announcement nothing has been heard of her.

Hundreds of coloured lanterns were hung in the trees to light the gardens after dark. These contained tightly packed slow burning gunpowder and had to be taken down, replenished and rehung nightly – an arduous task until the Hall became one of the first venues in Margate to have electricity.

Animals bred and trained by succeeding menagerie keepers were sent all over Europe and for years many circuses and zoos owned an animal named Margate. Some of the greatest successes were achieved by Capt George Sadlere who at times would be sharing his cottage in the grounds with up to 20 lion cubs who needed bottle feeding.

In 1899 Sadlere's animal husbandry resulted in an unusual pairing of a lion cub with a lamb and, after a spell on display in the gardens, they joined Sanger's Circus where a lion was always paraded on a tableau wagon crouched at the feet of a 'Britannia'. In those days of Empire, a lion and a lamb gave an added patriotic dimension.

Another leonine protegy was Emperor, christened by King Oscar of Sweden when Sadlere took the lion cub to a party on board the king's yacht at Ramsgate.

Emperor was taught to walk two tightropes stretched over the lake in the gardens. One night Emperor was startled by a firework display. He lost his balance, fell into the water, swam out and ran soaking wet to Sadlere's cottage!

5. Thought to have been taken in 1904, George Sadlere with Emperor, just one of the lions in his care.

First awakenings

When Sadlere married in October 1900 he and his bride Ellen cut their wedding cake in the lions' cage. A few of the guests boldly accepted the couple's invitation to join them and drink a toast with the lions beside them.

In 1905, aged nearly 80, Sanger sold his circus and the Hall's menagerie, dispersing the animals. The sale only raised £350, with Emperor accounting for £125. Sold to EH Bostock's menagerie in Glasgow, the lion pined for Sadler who later made the journey north of the border.

Sanger died tragically on 28 November 1911, aged 86. He had a large house at Finchley, north London, where he accused his manservant Herbert Cooper of stealing £50. A relation, Harry Austin, sacked Cooper and appointed a replacement named Jackson. Some weeks later Cooper entered the home and attacked Jackson with a razor. Austin dashed out from a nearby room where he had been reading to Sanger. Cooper rushed at Austin and felled him with a hatchet. Sanger rose from his chair to intervene, seizing a heavy candelabrum from the mantelpiece. Cooper knocked this aside causing it to fall heavily on to Sanger's head leaving him unconscious. Seeing what he had done Cooper leapt out of a window and ran off.

Although Sanger seemed to recover from the experience and to be none the worse during the evening, he died that night. Jackson was not seriously wounded while Austin was taken to hospital where he later recovered. Two days later Cooper's body was found on the Great Northern Railway between Highgate and Crouch End. Cooper had committed suicide.

Sanger's demise and subsequent funeral at Margate made national news. His polished oak coffin was brought from London to Margate on the train for the funeral on 11 December. In pouring rain silent and bareheaded crowds gathered on the seafront to watch the cortege make its way from the station to the town's cemetery, passing the Hall. A procession of 50 carriages made the solemn journey. The first three of these were almost covered by 123 floral emblems. The Margate side of the funeral was directed by Job Gore, one of the original Gore Brothers, whose firm still exists in Thanet.

6. Above: 'Lord' George Sanger c1900.
7. Left: A contemporary cameo of the great showman.
8. Below: The imposing Sanger family memorials at Margate Cemetery. It is brother John whose grave is expensively topped with a Mazeppa circus horse.

9. The cover from a 1913 souvenir programme showed there was much to enjoy at The Hall By The Sea, by then under the personal direction of Mr and Mrs Arthur Reeve.

Blinds were drawn and businesses closed – some all day – and cabbies had black bows tied to their whips. The cortege was met at the cemetery by the Mayor and entire town council with representatives from the dozen or more local organisations with which Sanger had associations.

10. Sanger's funeral cortege passes along Margate's Marine Terrace on 11 December 1911. The route to the cemetery was lined by hundreds of people.

Even in death the consummate showman provided Margate with a day of diversion.

Ownership of The Hall By The Sea had passed to Arthur and Harriet Reeve who worked at raising its appeal to the better class of holidaymaker otherwise attracted to Cliftonville and the Winter Gardens which opened in 1911.

The ballroom and dance programme included regular masquerades and costume balls. There were carnival novelty nights with prize competitions in the skating rink and fetes were held in the gardens. An old fashioned, genteel atmosphere was cultivated – notices at the seafront entrance read 'Close dancing, Turkey Trot, Bunny Hug or any other Negro freakish dances are strictly forbidden in this ballroom'.

The Hall By The Sea remained open throughout the First World War, albeit at a reduced level, but by 1919 the style of the business was becoming jaded. The Reeves, now in their sixties, decided it was time for a well earned retirement.

11. *It said Dreamland on the front of the building but the Hall By The Sea name is still visible on the side in this early 1920s view.*

Making the dream come true

At the end of November 1919 it was announced the Hall had been sold for £40,000 to a new owner. He was 47 year old John Henry Iles who arrived in Margate on the train one afternoon, looked around the site, wrote a cheque for the deposit during tea with the elderly couple and was on his way again – all in just two hours.

As the wealthy proprietor of an advertising agency, Iles had been able to indulge his passion for brass bands. He organised and sponsored festivals and edited a specialist magazine, The British Bandsman – but in 1906, while on world tour with a band, he was so impressed with the obvious profitability of American amusement parks he sold his business to a partner and launched into a new career.

During subsequent holidays in Margate, he decided The Hall By The Sea could be transformed into an American style amusement park and resolved to buy it.

He already had one of Britain's earliest Scenic Railways running at Blackpool's South Shore. He built another for the Franco-British Exhibition in London in 1908 and went on to develop complete amusement parks in cities around the world including Paris, Berlin, Barcelona and Pittsburgh, calling them after the two most

famous amusement parks at New York's Coney Island, either Luna Park or Dreamland.

It was this latter name that he chose for his new venture at Margate gradually phasing the old one out by using the title 'Dreamland Hall' for a few months.

Over the next 15 years Iles was to spend more than £500,000 developing Dreamland. To superintend the project he brought to Margate, as his works manager and engineer, Edmund Mancey who had been apprenticed to Magnus Volk and on whose experience of Volk's Railway at Brighton, Iles had been able to draw when he had first entered the amusement business.

Iles' initial move was to install a new floor in the ballroom, convert the old bar into a cocktail lounge and provide professional tuition in the latest tango dances by MC and manager Alan Clare.

The ballroom was 275 feet long and 55 feet wide. It was decorated throughout with mirrors on which were painted beautifully coloured animals and birds, and lined with ornamental trusses supporting over two dozen different statues.

The roof was hung with draperies and festoons. During the 1920s, stripped of most of this ornamentation it would become Dreamland's first cinema.

12. *An interior view of Dreamland's Palais de Danse recorded soon after John Henry Iles took over in late 1919. It would have looked similar during the Sanger era and was originally intended to be a railway station booking hall.*

13. *Statues in the gardens were said to be similarly styled to those in the Vatican City.*

Making the dream come true

14. *The Abbey ruins in the gardens were a folly originally built during Sanger's time but still looked impressive when photographed in the 1920s. This was a publicity shot used for a number of years in publicity brochures.*

15. *A view of the park c1925 showing, from left of centre, the Caterpillar, the main arcade and, on the right, the platform of the Scenic Railway. Beyond that lies the Racing Coaster. Judging by the hats and coats being worn, this wasn't the hottest day of the summer season.*

Dreamland, Margate

(TWO MINUTES FROM THE RAILWAY STATION)

PALAIS - DE - DANSE

Dancing Every Evening

In the GLORIOUS HALL OF MIRRORS. FULL LONDON ORCHESTRA.
Fully Licensed.

ADMISSION, 1/6. Except Special Carnival Nights, for details of which see other Bills.

Sunday Concerts

• Every Sunday Evening, FULL LONDON PROGRAMMES.
Many Famous Artistes Engaged.
Reserved Seats Booked in Advance at the Hall, or at Thornton Bobby's, Northdown Road, Cliftonville.

Musical Teas

The Hall is Open every Afternoon for TEAS & ICES, 2.30 to 5.30.
ADMISSION FREE.   FULL ORCHESTRA.   POPULAR PRICES.

Dreamland Park

The most Up-to-date Amusement Centre on the South Coast. Many Novel and Exciting Attractions. Delightful Tea Gardens. Magnificent Scenic Railway to be Opened shortly.

ADMISSION FREE !   ADMISSION FREE !

Zoological Gardens

Finest Collection of Wild Animals at any Seaside Resort. Completely re-organised.   Lions, Lionesses, Leopards, Pumas and Bears, with a host of others.   OPEN 10 TILL DUSK.

Clifton Baths Estate

(ALL TRAMS STOP AT THE ENTRANCE)

Clifton Cinema

Largest Screen and Largest Pictures in Margate. Fine Programme of Exclusive Films

Performances Daily, 2.45, 6.30 & 8.30.   POPULAR PRICES.

Clifton Concert Hall

Indoors and Outdoors combined.   LESLIE FULLER'S FAMOUS "PED'LER'S" CONCERT PARTY.   Twice Daily, 3.15 and 8 p.m.
Special Sunday Evening Concerts.

The Cliff Tea Gardens

Magnificent Sea Views.   Ideal conditions.

Swimming Bath

The only structure of its kind in Thanet. Sea Bathing with the chill off.

Warm Baths

The only Public Baths in Margate. Fresh or Sea Water Ozone Baths; a speciality widely recommended by the Medical Profession

Sea Bathing

A large number of well appointed Bathing Machines.
Attendants always present.

Ye Old English Fair

(NEAR THE PIER AND HARBOUR)

All the Fun of the Fair. Gaiety and Frolic from beginning to end.   Margate's Merriest Spot.

Dalby Square Sports Ground

Right on the Front, yet sheltered. Hard Tennis Courts specially constructed.

Clarke & Knapp, Printers, Margate.

16. A handbill from spring 1920 advertising some of the regular events to be held at Dreamland and the Clifton Baths Estate – which would later become the Lido, Cliftonville.

The gardens stayed as they were and were used for afternoon teas and concerts by Iles' beloved brass bands. Drainage of the adjoining fields commenced at once and by March 1920 the first stage in the development of the amusement park was begun on approximately the top half of the site.

It would be another 10 years before the lower half could be used for more than firework displays and as a football pitch by Margate Football Club whose home ground it had been since September 1912.

A Joy Wheel, a Haunted Castle, a House of Nonsense, a Cake Walk, a Helter Skelter and numerous sideshows greeted the first visitors to Dreamland on its opening day on 3 July 1920. The Dreamland Miniature Railway was completed just in time and firework displays by the firm Brock & Co were planned.

Even so there was still an air of sparseness as a result of a post war shortage of materials, limited time, money and the need for lighter constructed buildings because of the ground conditions.

The Joy Wheel was brought from the Clifton Baths Estate at Cliftonville and rebuilt in the park. On this contraption up to 20 people sat for a circular ride. As it got faster and faster they would start to fall off, till only one was left. These first attractions would be enhanced the following year by a Lunar Ball – Britain's first – and two other rides which had only previously been seen at London's Olympia, The Whip and The Tumble Bug.

Back then, as it would be for so long, it was the Scenic Railway which was the centrepiece. This mammoth construction of Canadian douglas fir cost more than £20,000 and, with a track length of nearly a mile, was one of the largest of its kind.

Iles had obtained the European rights on Scenic Railways building them at a number of British and Continental amusement parks before the First World War – so it was an easy decision to build another in Margate.

The Scenic Railway was an instant hit. In the 13 weeks of the remaining summer season it carried more than half a million delighted passengers. In 1921, its first full season, it carried nearly a million and helped prompt Iles to form Dreamland Ltd, which had a capital of £75,000, in September of this year. Local residents as well as members of his family were invited to buy shares.

17. *Sedate Devonshire cream teas could be enjoyed in the shadow of the Scenic Railway when the park first opened in 1920.*

Even on the day before the official opening hundreds had packed on to the Scenic's trains when it operated for charity. The takings were duly presented to the Mayor of Margate, Alderman Alonzo Pilcher, for the Cottage Hospital fund at a formal celebration lunch held in the Hall of Mirrors. This local dignitary actually received a large bag of cash – no giant sized cheques in those days!

During his speech at the lunch, Iles said he believed, correctly as it turned out, that Dreamland would have an important bearing on the future prosperity of Margate. More varied entertainments than the borough yet offered would prove greatly advantageous and increase the popularity and prosperity of the resort.

The success of the Scenic Railway, whose profits alone were reckoned to be enough to pay the debenture holders in the new Margate Estates holding company, would encourage the later construction of a similar but gentler ride – the Racing Coaster. These two car trains ran on castors rather than rails and were guided on their journey by rubbing boards.

A week after the opening the Isle of Thanet Gazette reported: "Visitors and residents who flocked to Dreamland Hall and Gardens have been astonished at the metamorphosis created by the army of workmen throughout the winter and spring.

18. *Advertisement from the Isle of Thanet Gazette announcing Dreamland's impending opening.*

and Co., Ltd., for the "GRAND CAFE" and sold at their London Prices.
TABLES RESERVED. 'Phone: 63 Margate.

DREAMLAND PARK,

MARGATE,

Will be Opened to the Public

ON

SATURDAY, JULY 3rd.

It will provide the most fascinating up-to-date and enjoyable

AMUSEMENTS CENTRE

In the Isle of Thanet.

Its attractions include

Giant Scenic Railway
Joy Wheel
Haunted Castle
House of Nonsense
Miniature Railway

And a host of other THRILLING, EXCITING, and INTERESTING EVENTS.

SATURDAY, JULY 3rd.

THE BEST

19. Dreamland's Miniature Railway, designed by Henry Greenly, featured on an early 1920s postcard.

"The great Scenic Railway has at once captivated the public imagination and its trains have been running in almost ceaseless succession.

"The zoo has been brought up to date and many new animals added. An enormous kitchen has been constructed, making it possible to cater for holiday parties of 1,500, besides providing for the regular daily demand."

Another popular attraction was the Miniature Railway. Its 15 inch gauge rails ran for 600 yards around the park, over two lattice steel bridges, under a third, across a five span wooden viaduct and a level crossing. There was also a loco shed and a station complete with coal store

20. As the track length of the Miniature Railway was shortened to make way for more new rides so the main station had to be rebuilt – in the Modernist style of the era – and an engine traverser installed.

Making the dream come true

21. The Miniature Railway was created from scratch in around three months during spring 1920 for the park's opening in July. The 'Little Giant' class engine Prince Edward of Wales, was built some years before by Bassett-Lowke.

and signals, adjoining a new secondary entrance to the park at Eaton Road away from the seafront. Construction of this elaborate little track was led by well known miniature railway engineer Henry Greenly (later knighted) who went on to build the Romney Hythe & Dymchurch Railway with its owner Captain John Howey.

Dreamland's first locomotive was Prince Edward of Wales, built in 1908. It was delivered from Rhyl in north Wales with six coaches. Billie, the second and larger engine, arrived in late 1922. Like so many steam engines they had personalities of their own and were revered by visitors and staff for many years.

The construction of the Miniature Railway was a major development in its own right for enthusiasts and was given significant coverage in the August and September 1920 issues of The Model Engineer and Electrician magazine.

As more rides were brought to the park in successive years so the track was reduced until it was about half its original length but the attraction was given a new station complete with engine traverser to ease shunting after each round trip.

22. The gardens looked particularly tranquil in the 1920s with a river running through the middle.

23. *A trainload of Scenic Railway passengers turn for the camera before heading around the one mile course sometime in the 1920s. Riders were expected to stay firmly seated without safety belts or restraints.*

24. *The rocky man made mountain facade of Over The Falls and the Rapids tower behind it were a dominant part of the view across the park during its formative years.*

25. Repeat rides on the Scenic Railway were only 6d when this view, showing the original arcade, was taken c1925.

26. Looking towards the railway line at the rear of the park, the Racing Coaster is on the left, the Great Whirlwind in the centre while on the right are the zoo buildings in this 1923 view. Extreme right is one end of the Scenic Railway.

27. The Caterpillar soon after arrival in 1922 showing the covers rolled only halfway.

1922 saw the introduction of The Caterpillar. Iles had bought the sole European rights for this ride the previous year, thus making it another ride always associated with Dreamland. For many years he ran Caterpillars at a number of British and Continental amusement parks, each the subject of an individual operating company. Dreamland's Caterpillar would last longest until the early 1980s.

Countless thousands were whisked round an 80 feet diameter undulating track at increasing speed, suddenly plunged into darkness by a cover and startled by wailing Klaxons. After a few minutes the hood would be just as suddenly folded back to coincide with a blast of compressed air blown under each rider, often raising ladies' skirts right over their heads – much to the hilarity of numerous bystanders.

28. A 1923 scene of the park with the Racing Coaster ride, in its first season, centre stage. The coaster would thrill millions for more than half a century. To the left is The Biff ride while on the right is the Great Whirlwind ride.

29. The front of the River Caves can be clearly seen in this 1920s view when the park started to take on a more uniform appearance. The giant Haunted Snail proved to be a memorable, if not scary, feature for many years until lost in a fire in June 1957. The snail originally cost concessionaire Sara Hastings £4,000 to build.

The Coaster Railway, better known as the Racing Coaster was a new addition to the park in 1923, costing 'between eight and nine thousand pounds'. Contemporary publicity describes the coaster thus: "It is one of the fastest rides possible. It has those quick little dips which tickle you so."

The promotional brochure 'What's On At Dreamland' was distributed widely during the summer seasons of the 1920s and in one section it gives an outline of how large a concern the park had become.

It said: "It requires a lot of foresight to deal with 30,000 people a day who pass in and out. On firework nights alone there are often more than 12,000 people in the park at one time.

"There is a good deal of risk with many amusements. It is curious what takes the public's fancy. Sometimes one puts up a show costing thousands of pounds and yet is it is not successful. Perhaps some small detail is altered which makes all the difference and one has difficulty in coping with the number of patrons."

The Empire Exhibition at the then all new Wembley stadium in 1924 was the source of the third of Dreamland's longest lasting rides – The River Caves, demolished in 1984. Colloquially known as The Tubs, passengers sat in huge metal bins gliding along a swift flowing waterway through a series of plaster and cement constructed caves.

These included the Ice Cave, the Smugglers' Cave and the Venetian Cave. A sedate ride, its basic wooden construction and primitive waterwheel mechanism meant it required even more maintenance than the Scenic Railway. Although aimed mainly at a family audience, many a romantic couple would take advantage of the dark seclusion it provided.

30. Anticipation is the title of this early 1920s photo in the zoo. A tasty fish proves irresistible for this aquatic bird – much to the amusement of the gathered throng!

31. A 1920s postcard gives a good view of the Caterpillar ride and, further back, the Motor Racing Cars which could be enjoyed for 6d a time. In among the sideshows behind is the Haunted House which offered 'a devil of a good time!'

DREAMLAND POPULAR RESTAURANT

SPECIAL TO-DAY

Fish & Chips	8d
Two Fillets of Plaice & Chips.	10d
Two Large Fillets & Chips.	1/-
Steak & Chips.	1/6d
Chump Chop & Chips.	1/6d
Ham & Two Eggs.	1/3d
One Egg & Chips.	6d
Two Eggs & Chips.	10d
One Sausage & Mashed Potatoes.	6d
Two Sausages & Mashed Potatoes.	9d
Onions.	2d

Fish & Chips wrapped in carrier Bags for taking away 1d extra. Customers are requested to compare their bill with the menu. Any complaint of incivility made to the management will be esteemed a favour.

Worthington

The Perfect BEER

Typical prices for rides were 6d for a turn on the Scenic Railway, 4d for the Racing Coaster and the same for a spin on the Caterpillar. Coveted books of free ride tickets, endorsed by Edmund Mancey, now park manager, were offered to those who had helped the management in some way – but were valid only on weekdays.

For those in need of sustenance in the park, the Dreamland Popular restaurant was close to hand in one corner and here visitors could dine out at 'moderate prices'. The Popular's menu offered fish and chips for 8d (4p), steak and chips or chump chop and chips for 1/6d (7.5p) each while sausage and mash could be scoffed for a mere 6d (2.5p). Carrier bags for taking fish and chips away were offered for a penny extra. For those who wanted a dessert, cherry tart and custard was available for 6d (2.5p) or boiled sultana roll for just 4d (2p).

Customer service was clearly important for the menus also suggested: "Customers are requested to compare their bill with the menu. Any complaint of incivility made to the management will be esteemed a favour."

32. Menu card setting out the fare at the park's Popular Restaurant in 1928.

Making the dream come true

Tragedy struck the park on 15 June 1928 when four people were killed – Dreamland's first fatalities – as a newly installed ride came apart one afternoon.

The German made Atlantic Flyer consisted of eight flying boats, each able to carry eight people. The boats were suspended on steel struts and rotated in roundabout style. A metal bolt at the end of one of the boat's struts broke, tilting the craft and flinging its occupants in all directions 20 feet below.

Three Londoners were among the dead, Frank Lane, 16, Walter Humphreys, 22, Philip Finkelstein, 20, who died in hospital later, and Horace John Death, 40, a local drayman, were named at an inquest in Margate the following Monday. Four more people were treated for head and leg injuries.

At the inquest, the coroner, Mr G Camfield, was told two of the victims had their necks broken and the others died from skull fractures.

The flyer's owner Fritz Schmidt, an experienced fairground operator, was mortified by the incident. He spoke in a shaky voice at the inquest and broke down several times.

The coroner decided the four victims had died through misadventure. Mr Schmidt later sold on the ride, asking people 'to refrain from making unreasonable offers as my nerves are shattered' in his advertisement in the World's Fair trade newspaper.

It's interesting to note how quickly the formalities of the accident were dealt with in the days before health and safety issues achieved their notoriety. The inquest was held a few days after the event and the cause was known almost right away. No further action appears to have been taken against Dreamland or Fritz Schmidt. Blame appears not to have been apportioned either.

In national coverage of the accident, the Daily Sketch shows a picture of the ride, stating the numbers killed and in the same caption points out the newspaper is able to offer its readers free accident insurance!

In 1929 visitors to Dreamland were able to enjoy the additional benefit of being able to see the Home Life Exhibition held in the park's exhibition hall between July 8 and August 31. Clearly intended as a smaller scale Ideal Home Exhibition,

33. A busy day in the park shows the Winchester Rifle range, centre, and the roundabout in full use.

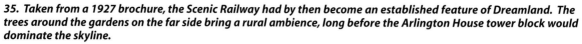

34. *One of the earliest known pictures of the Scenic Railway, taken during its first full season in 1921 when the trains carried one million passengers. It was published in a 1922 brochure promoting Dreamland's British Industries exhibition.*

35. *Taken from a 1927 brochure, the Scenic Railway had by then become an established feature of Dreamland. The trees around the gardens on the far side bring a rural ambience, long before the Arlington House tower block would dominate the skyline.*

36. *The gardens brought a calming influence to the park in the 1920s.*

37. *A team of maintenance men ensures one of the Scenic Railway's trains is kept in good order in 1930. The photo was taken by distinguished Fleet Street photographer James Jarché who would, a few years later, be the first to get a picture of King Edward VIII with the then unidentified American divorcée Wallis Simpson.*

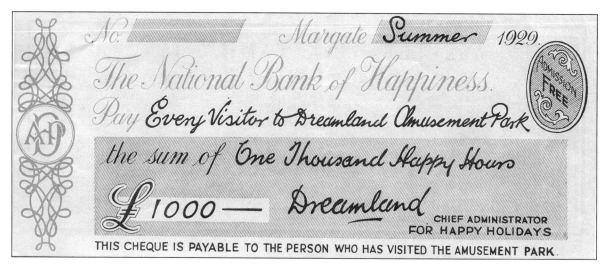

No.   *Margate*   **Summer**   *1929*

The National Bank of Happiness.

Pay   *Every Visitor to Dreamland Amusement Park*

the sum of One Thousand Happy Hours

£ 1000 —   *Dreamland*

ADMISSION FREE

CHIEF ADMINISTRATOR
FOR HAPPY HOLIDAYS

THIS CHEQUE IS PAYABLE TO THE PERSON WHO HAS VISITED THE AMUSEMENT PARK.

38. A lucky number cheque from Dreamland's National Bank of Happiness could win the holder the princely sum of £5 in 1929. The promotion ran for several seasons in the late 1920s and winning numbers were posted by the Scenic Railway every Friday. The first prize is equivalent to nearly £200 in today's money.

a brochure published to entice standholders states: "The exhibition, the largest and most important in the South of England, is being organised to bring before the public all those many items of domestic necessity and comfort which form such an important part of every home."

The event displayed everything for the drawing room, dining room, bedroom, kitchen, garden, recreation, amusement and instruction. Attractions would be of interest to every housewife and family man, promised the guide in its effusive tone. There's no surviving evidence to

39. Sandwich board men prepare to walk around Margate advertising Dare Devil Peggy, a one legged high diver, in 1930. Peggy would dive 60 feet into a small tank of water.

40. Wreckage of the 1930 fire which claimed a number of rides, sideshows and a roundabout. Note the two firemen examining the wreckage.

suggest how successful the idea would be but stand prices ranged from £15 per week for the largest down to £4 per week for the smallest – worth £550 and £160 respectively in today's money, so there would have to have been plenty of sales leads generated to justify the outlay!

The park had seen a fair amount of restructuring as the 1930s arrived – mainly out of necessity owing to a damaging fire. A combination of wooden buildings erected throughout the 1920s and widespread cigarette smoking was a recipe for disaster. In September 1930, the central arcade – one of the old aircraft hangars – caught fire completely destroying sideshows housed therein. Several nearby rides such as the Rapids and Over The Falls also disappeared in the inferno. More than £20,000 worth of damage was caused in little over an hour.

The Isle of Thanet Gazette reported the blaze had started soon after park closing time at 11pm and the fire brigade had arrived within a couple of minutes. Flames shot up to 120 feet high and could be seen for miles around, drawing an estimated crowd of 5,000 to watch the drama unfold.

There were no serious injuries – a pet greyhound named Sweet Dolly, chained up in an office by the Haunted House, was released by police.

The newspaper robustly refuted national media claims that firemen ran short of water and had to pump sea water on to the flames instead. The Eaton Road hydrant had proved sufficient, said the Gazette, and it was business as normal the following day with the remaining attractions in operation.

Arising from the ashes the following year was a brand new concrete structured arcade, much larger and better than before. A contemporary brochure showing an artist's impression of the building promised it would bring patrons 'pleasure without measure'. The new arcade was 'a vast improvement, embracing new ideas,

41. The arcade and nearby rides were well alight when this dramatic scene was captured of the 1930 blaze.

42. *The new arcade was ready for the 1931 season and looks imposing with the Motor Boats ride in the foreground.*

new degrees of comfort, entertainment and amusement'.

Its entrances were indeed grand, standing at about 30 or 40 feet high, and echoing the trendy Modernist style of the time. However, at second glance beyond those frontages the structure was utilitarian, with corrugated iron or asbestos sheets providing the external covering.

Close by a Motor Boats ride was introduced. 'A dozen or so stout speedy little motor craft, each with a happy holidaymaker at the helm, chase one another round the attractively laid out and winding waterway', said a brochure of the time.

43. *The Motor Boats ride itself, fun to navigate around its winding course and fun to watch from the footbridge over.*

44. The Brooklands Racers, seen here in 1931, appear crudely styled compared to later versions driven around the track.

The chance to replace other wooden structures in the vicinity was also taken and along with newly laid out gardens and flower beds the park took on a more unified and tidier appearance.

The fire had proved to be a turning point for the park, with the management declaring it had 'courageously made this great misfortune the opportunity for creating a new and even more original park, with every amenity and excitement to welcome and make happy its visitors'. Dreamland boasted it had the largest ballroom on the south coast, the most beautiful gardens and the loveliest shaded promenades as well as the park itself.

Fire struck again early one morning in August 1937 destroying staff rooms and workshops. Fifty waitresses lost their uniforms and a season's tips, leaving a few almost penniless. The blaze spread to a paint store, gutted a glass-cutting room, the plumber's department, bill posting and publicity rooms as well as wrecking a store containing weekly magazines belonging to Amalgamated Press.

Strong winds fanned the flames towards the firework store, setting off some of the smaller varieties. Larger set pieces were untouched, still enabling that week's display to go ahead.

45. John Henry Iles is pictured, front right, as the Mayor and Mayoress of Margate, Percy Osborne and his wife, officially open the new arcade in 1931.

46. Another picture by James Jarché shows the Trainair flight simulator in 1930. Biplanes were still common at the time but this ride was foretelling the future with a scaled down monoplane instead.

47. Donkey derbys were very popular as this 1933 scene shows – perhaps not so popular with the animals who could be kept hard at it on a busy summer's day. Beaver and Tuppence are the names of the donkeys nearest the camera.

48. In what is clearly a publicity photo, a couple of young women are drafted in to help one of the electricians ensure all is in working order in the park's Garden of Light in the 1930s. Note also the Nestlé 1d chocolate bar machine.

49. Right: An early 1930s handbill delivered in its thousands to holidaymakers to Thanet. The rides, weekly fireworks and nightly dancing were all on offer.

50. Below: A 1934 view inside the buffet building which was open to the left hand side, where thousands would have refreshed themselves with cups of tea, meat pies and plates of chips! Prices were 'cheap and competitive' according to adverts of the period.

YOU Must Visit
DREAMLAND
MARGATE,
RIGHT ON THE SEA FRONT
ALL TRAMS AND BUSES PASS ENTRANCES

Amusement Park
ADMISSION FREE. OPEN SUNDAYS

HOSTS OF ATTRACTIONS!

SCENIC RAILWAY, WHIRLWIND RACING COASTER, OVER THE FALLS, CATERPILLAR, RIVER CAVES, SKOOTER, TUMBLE BUG, MINIATURE RAILWAY, BEAUTIFUL FLOWER GARDENS AND ZOO.

Restaurants, Cafes and Buffets

SUPER CINEMA
(100% TALKIES, VARIETIES, FULL ORCHESTRA AND NEW ORGAN)

And .. Magnificent BALLROOM DANCING NIGHTLY

FIREWORKS
EVERY THURSDAY Admission 6d. Children 3d.

John Waddington Ltd., Leeds : and London.

51. The Garden Café, largest of Dreamland's restaurants, laid up for 1,200 people in 1928.

Two airship hangars had been playing an important part in Dreamland's development for several years by now. Measuring 200 feet long, they had originally been ordered by the US Coastguard Service during the First World War but with the end of hostilities in 1918 they had become surplus to requirements. After some negotiation they arrived in Margate in kit form for assembly.

52. Lightning service was a proud boast of the well equipped and staffed kitchens.

One housed an arcade of an increasing number of stalls and sideshows – the one that burned down in 1930 – while the other provided the shell of what became known as the Garden Café.

This was capable of seating up to 1,200 people – easily the largest of seven, and later eight, restaurants around the park. These were the heydays of the works and factory beanfeast outings. Dozens of charabancs, and later streamlined motor coaches, would disgorge their passengers in Dreamland's own coach park. Those arriving on specially chartered trains only had a short stroll from the station before reaching their destination. In its quest to ensure all went smoothly for a firm's outing to Dreamland – the management was not very keen to mention much else about Margate – visitors were also directed to take advantage of Southern Railway's offer of the return journey at single fare price for groups of eight or more.

Special efforts were made to attract mid week parties – particularly children – to the park. Separate brochures were printed for those interested. It was after all, quite easy to bring in weekend trade – when three times the numbers which could be accepted were turned away – but weekdays were usually quieter. As an incentive for midweek groups, every person in 1932 was given two free tickets for any of the park's rides. Worth having when a go on the Scenic Railway was 6d a time.

53. Members of a 1923 outing pose for a group photo outside the cinema entrance. Note the entertainers sat in the centre of the front row.

The literature assured group secretaries: "The old fun fair image is a thing of the past – Dreamland is a park of the exhibition standard." Indeed it was.

Keen to ratchet up the competition against other major English seaside resorts, Margate's borough council was happy to provide cards comparing the rainfall and sunshine the town had against places including Bournemouth, Torquay, Eastbourne and Brighton. Needless to say Margate came out on top, enjoying an average 6.23 hours of sun every day between April and September. Only Eastbourne came

54. Dreamland catering promised everything from a simple meal to a banquet in the 1920s and 1930s.

A simple meal or a banquet – Dreamland can offer it to you at a price unequalled, and a service unexcelled.

Eight fully licensed halls are available for every kind and size of party, and over 3,500 can be seated at one time.

For 15 years Dreamland has specialized in catering for Outing parties.

close with 5.98 hours. Barely more than 13 inches of rain fell in the same period, with Eastbourne again closest at 16 inches.

Mass catering would remain an important part of Dreamland's business for 30 years and it was common for parties of several hundred to sit down for lunch together. All told, the restaurants could accommodate 3,500 people. In the early 1930s Dreamland's claim to be the largest caterer in the country was entirely justified with more than 130,000 customers a year. The catering manager John Forbes earned an enviable reputation as a result.

All this feeding and watering demanded a large team to ensure everything was served on time. Accordingly, there were three well equipped kitchens, a butchery, bakery and an ice factory. Teams of chefs provided 'lightning service' the management claimed in its brochures of the day. Dreamland's bakery was producing 2,500 fancy cakes and over 2,000 loaves each day during the high season while the ice cream plant turned out 80 gallons on a hot day.

Hot lunches started at three shillings and sixpence a head (18p) and included soup, with a choice of roast beef and Yorkshire pudding or roast mutton with vegetables. Dessert choices were fruit tart and custard sauce or jelly.

55. This is the Popular restaurant laid up for a lunch party of 550 people in 1935.

56. Just some idea of how much food was eaten by beanfeasters at the height of summers in the 1920s.

FACTS

What do people eat when they come to Dreamland?

Here at least, are some details of the havoc wrought by visitors in the various Dreamland Restaurants in the 4 months of last season: Our visitors consumed:

50 TONS OF POTATOES

14 TONS OF BEEF MUTTON AND LAMB

5 TONS OF HAM

10 TONS OF FISH

1½ TONS OF TEA

5 TONS OF SUGAR

3000 GALLONS OF ICE CREAM

We catered for over 80,000 people in parties, and this number does *not* include the many thousands of our casual and unattached visitors.

A feature of last year's working was the remarkable increase of small outing parties consisting of 10 to 30 people.

For those paying the top six shillings each (30p) the choice widened to offer fried fillet of sole or roast lamb or chicken. In 1931, these delights could be washed down with a bottle of white wine from four shillings and sixpence (23p) or a bottle of beer – Guinness, pale ale or milk stout – at sevenpence halfpenny each (about 4p). A bottle of quality champagne was priced at 18 shillings (90p).

A party of 741 people from a brewery in Southwark, south east London, was among the many satisfied customers.

The grateful secretary wrote: "I enclose the company's cheque for £276 1s 4d in settlement of your account for meals supplied. The men thoroughly enjoyed their outing and were very satisfied with the catering arrangements. If we come to Margate again, we shall certainly enquire whether we can be accommodated at Dreamland before trying elsewhere."

Quite what any ladies thought of their visit is unknown – perhaps wisely, they went elsewhere or stayed at home that day!

Until the early fifties Dreamland made all its own ice cream which was also sold wholesale to hotels and shops, together with the wrappers and spoons. Also its own bread and cakes could be bought by the public from a small shop at the front of the bakery. The wrapped Dreamland loaf became famous and was produced for resale around the district.

57. Inside Dreamland's first cinema during the silent era of the 1920s.

As early as 1923 it was decided to capitalise on the booming silent movie business by converting the ballroom into a 900 seat cinema. This opened on 17 May with a 13 piece orchestra providing the music and sound effects for Hall Caine's great epic of the era – The Prodigal Son. The addition a few months later of a small stage enabled variety acts such as Ken and Mac – twa draps o' Scotch – and Raglas the international juggler to also appear in what was then called the Dreamland Variety Cinema.

At the same time the old roller skating rink was transformed into a large ballroom with a Tudor style decoration and a mosaic marble floor.

It was named the Palais de Danse and carnival nights were held on Thursdays and Saturdays. Creating the Variety cinema and converting the roller rink into the ballroom cost £20,000, a serious sum of money for the period.

The cinema showed all the latest 'super films' – then still silent – with a full London orchestra providing accompanying music. Performances were held at 10.45am if wet, as well as at 2.30pm, 6.15pm and 10.30pm.

The original Compton Noterman organ, dating from the opening of the building 36 years earlier, was restored by August 1929. Celebrated organist and composer Gatty Sellers was the first to perform on the revamped instrument, which featured two manual keyboards and 17 straight units. The following April talkies were introduced.

Despite all this work on the cinema it became obvious within a few years it could not compete with others nearby, namely the Astoria and Regal. Both had been earmarked as super cinemas to stand out from the other old fashioned establishments around the town at the time.

Margate Estates' management decided a project ambitious enough to be the last word in comfort and style was required. An era of skyscrapers, neon lights, positive features and bold use of glass had arrived. Work would begin at the end of the 1933 summer season.

58. An isometric drawing of part of the new building as shown in Building magazine, June 1934. It carried an extensive feature on the work in hand.

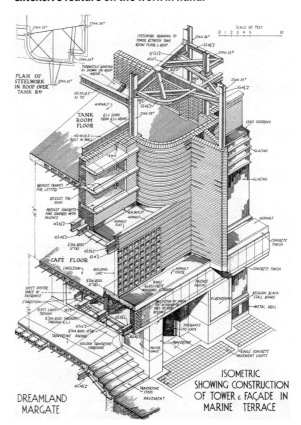

Distinguished architects Julian Leathart and WF Granger were commissioned to design a new entertainment complex containing a super cinema, ballroom, restaurant, bars and lounges.

Such was the size and complexity of the scheme that the plans and drawings soon appeared in architectural journals, influencing the style of many more similar structures for years after.

Leathart and Granger were to be assisted by John Bird Iles, John Henry's 27 year old second son, an interior designer in his own right. John Bird Iles – his middle name was his mother's maiden name – was responsible for the elegant scheme of polished Australian wood dado surrounding the auditorium with sea gods and nymphs set into the walls – a sentimental link with the statues around the walls of the old Hall By The Sea which had previously stood on the site.

Work on the new building continued through the winter of 1934 and by the Whitsun holiday the Sunshine Café was open for business. Offering panoramic views over Margate seafront, it was able to seat 500 people. An additional benefit of this was that it could easily be turned into a much needed eighth dining room for beano parties.

In a specially produced progress report outlining 'The effects of the big improvements' the description said the company had been able to buy a strip of land from the council adjoining Dreamland which enabled the side road leading to the park to be widened by 50 per cent. This is probably what we know today as Hall By The Sea Road.

Work halted once the café had opened to allow the park's summer season to continue unhindered. It recommenced on 23 September with building the massive auditorium of the cinema and the adjoining maple floored ballroom.

Sadly, only a month before, the cinema's flamboyant manager Jack Binns had died on 4 August after a short illness. He had been in charge since 1925 after managing the town's

59. The frontage of Dreamland cinema in 1933, just before it was demolished to make way for the new complex.

Making the dream come true

60. An aerial view of Margate and Dreamland captured during the early 1930s – after the arcade was built but preceding the cinema and ballroom complex.

Hippodrome Theatre. The cinema closed for the afternoon of his funeral and the procession passed as close as possible to the building by crossing to the opposite side. Taking Jack's place was Harold Finch.

As construction continued, it became clear there were special problems to be overcome. Tons of earth were laid over sand and reinforced piling was driven up to 30 feet into the ground. A 60 ton steel balcony girder was installed to take the weight of the auditorium as it stretched over the access road into the park, allowing sufficient height for vehicles to pass underneath.

No expense was spared on the project and the cinema was designed to be one of the finest 'in the provinces'. Two large lounges, one for the stalls and the other for the circle, measuring 70 x 45 feet ensured a relaxing atmosphere and naturally bars were attached. Elsewhere, existing saloon and public bars were redecorated and extended, stretching back an extra 20 feet, while a new cellar restaurant was created from a small and narrow lounge below them.

"These reconstructions will make Dreamland the most up to date entertainment centre in the south and will provide a building of which the town can be justly proud. One cannot even estimate the benefit which this will give to the company's existing enterprises both in revenue and prestige," said the improvements brochure.

The project proved to be a triumph for Leathart and Granger but it would be their last joint venture in cinema design. Their 16 year long partnership was, however, dissolved by mutual consent in 1937. In that time they had designed schools and private residences but only a total of seven cinemas, remarkable considering the effect their work had on hundreds of others, particularly Odeons, as they sprang up around the country. Odeon's Birmingham based drawing office lost little time in borrowing Leathart and Granger's ideas and these were at their most obvious in cinemas built at Sutton Coldfield and Scarborough.

The cinema and ballroom building was completed in the early part of 1935 and was officially opened on 22 March. The final bill for the work came to £250,000 – more than £10 million in today's money – making it one of the biggest investments that Margate and Dreamland had ever seen, which was exactly what the management had intended.

The opening night souvenir programme of March 1935 notes that Margate's new super cinema was fully air-conditioned by a complex system of fans. Some 20 miles of heavy duty electrical cable were installed along with two acres of carpet and linoleum. The building also used 1.5 million bricks, 700 tons of cement and four acres of plaster as well as one and a half acres of glass.

61. *An artist's impression of how the new cinema would look at night from the seafront was used in Dreamland publicity material until the early 1970s. Note the Germanic spelling 'Kinema' on the frontage.*

62. *Inside the new Sunshine Café in 1934 offering a panoramic view of Margate seafront.*

Making the dream come true

63. Builders hadn't quite finished work when this view of the cinema building was taken. Note the lines of the Isle of Thanet Electric Tramway embedded in the road surface. These would be lifted in 1937 when trams ceased operations. Local gossip a few years later suggested the metal had been sold to scrap dealers from Germany and it then found its way back to Margate courtesy of the Luftwaffe!

The fin style outline frontage of the building was 80 feet high, ensuring it would be the tallest on Margate seafront until eclipsed by Arlington House nearly 30 years later. One or two of the labourers prided themselves on being able to climb to the very top to sunbathe on the narrowest part of the structure, just wide enough to lie down on!

The opening night itself was a grand occasion. Invited guests enjoyed a sumptuous buffet of champagne and oysters before Thanet MP Capt Harold Balfour carried out the formal opening. Later, he would find fame as a member of Winston Churchill's war cabinet and, later, as the first Baron of Inchrye after the Second World War.

64. *The impressive interior of Dreamland cinema in 1935. This photo was still being used to promote the place in the late 1960s and, below 65. The Art Deco foyer with the distinctive ticket booth, centre, and the front entrance doors to the right. The entire building was awarded rare Grade II* listing status in 2008.*

Settling down to watch the evening's screen entertainment in new comfy tip up seats the night's screen entertainment started off, in time honoured fashion with a B movie, in this case Laurel and Hardy's Them Thar Hills, followed by a Movietone newsreel and the main feature staring Greta Garbo in her latest film The Painted Veil. Arguably not one of her best it was nonetheless enjoyed by the audience of civic heads and dignitaries.

It's worth noting that items in the newsreel included stories about Germany asserting its right to rearm and, in contrast, London's police horses being readied for the King and Queen's royal silver jubilee celebrations that year as well another about the French liner Normandie, then the largest ship afloat.

A coveted copy of the opening night's souvenir programme notes: "The policy of Dreamland has assured its success. It might be summed up as 'The bringing of happiness to the many at a price they can afford. Giving ever better value, if possible at a diminishing cost. A vast turnover made this practicable. Yet price is not everything, since quality equally plays its part."

66. Another view inside the Sunshine Café.

67. The capacious interior of the cinema showing stalls and circle. In the 1970s, the circle would become two cinemas.

68. Even the stairways were designed to be elegant as well as functional. This one led up to the Sunshine Café.

The same programme thoughtfully adds in its general information that dog owners may leave their pets in special accommodation with an attendant. Quite how successful that was, is not known, but not difficult to visualise!

Outside, a smartly dressed commissionaire greeted patrons as they arrived. Ten usherettes saw people to their seats. Stalls were priced at 6d (2.5p), 9d (4p), one shilling (5p) and one and

69. Described as the cinema's saloon bar, the interior looks opulent fitted out in mock Tudor style.

six (7.5p). For the more affluent, balcony seats were priced at one and six and two shillings (10p). Pink carpets lined the foyer floors with blue settees and easy chairs dotted around to bring a relaxing, stylish ambience. Glass and pottery ashtrays were provided – but all of these had disappeared within a week.

In those days, no cinema was complete without its organ and organist which would rise majestically through the floor on a lift before every performance. Lewis Gerard was maestro of the many keyboards of Dreamland's Compton which had cost £4,850 to install. Somewhat inevitably the song Meet Me Tonight in Dreamland quickly became his signature tune. Within a few months Lewis was as much a star there as the Hollywood screen actors who followed after his performances.

Speaking of those days when he returned to Margate in 1972 for a concert, he recalled: "I had a horror of two things – talking to the audience and raising the organ lift for my performances. To my mind, they were never very reliable. At the final rehearsal on the night before the opening ceremony, I had concluded my solo and turned around to say something to Eric Iles when 'wham' – down the organ went about 14 feet – and fast. Fortunately no one was hurt and there was no damage to the organ. Eric Iles was unbelievable, he never flapped and just peered over the top of the orchestra rail and asked: 'Are you in distress?' You know, I couldn't even answer him."

The organ typifies the Art Deco style of those years, housed in a jelly mould collection of illuminated coloured glass panels. The console has four manual keyboards, 215 stops, a waterfall effect in the illuminated panels and, a revelation for the mid thirties, sounds to control a solo cello and percussion effects such as glockenspiel, xylophone, drums and cymbals – all of these housed in five rooms above the stage. The organ could also control a grand piano standing on the stage. A visual device called the Brenograph created a kaleidoscope of coloured designs on the screen.

Just as going to the pictures once or twice a week was a popular activity, so too was dancing in Dreamland's capacious ballroom. As part of the major development, every effort had been made to ensure people would enjoy themselves in glamorous surroundings – and prove profitable for the owners.

In a time when being able to fox trot, waltz, rumba, quick step and many more were considered social graces and not confined to celebrity TV shows on Saturday evenings, the ballroom was well used and able to cope with 500 couples dancing the night away together. A typical week's programme of the era would include a balloon and streamer carnival night, a mystery night, a special event to raise money for a local cause like the hospital and, at season's end, a farewell night to the band, often in the 1930s Harry Roy and His Lyricals. Dancing works up quite a thirst of course and drinks in the ballroom bar ranged from fourpence halfpenny for a pint of George Beer & Rigden's ales and stouts, 8d for a glass of sherry or a measure of spirits such as Nicholson's gin. From the soda fountain, fruit flavoured sodas were also 8d each. Admission to the ballroom depended on the event but was usually two shillings (10p) per person.

The successful career of John Henry Iles, by now the company chairman, came to an abrupt end in February 1938. He had invested heavily in a film production company making movie shorts, some starring comedian Leslie Fuller who had graduated to film stardom after appearing with his concert party at Cliftonville's Clifton Baths.

Iles had spent £250,000 of his own money rebuilding the Rock Studios at Elstree – thought to be the ones now used by the BBC to make programmes including Eastenders – but the venture was a complete disaster and he was left owing £351,000, a massive sum for the period equivalent to nearly £15 million in today's money.

70. Organist Lewis Gerard, pictured after his return in 1947, became an instant star of the cinema.

71. *A cheery photo of the motorboats captured in the mid 1930s – which would be still be in use 30 years later.*

72. *Smiles all round on this handbill from 1936.*

Happiness like this
means "Dreamland"
for you!

MARGATE'S
WONDER
AMUSEMENT PARK

FIREWORKS EVERY THURSDAY
and
HARRY ROY'S LYRICALS in THE GREAT BALLROOM

Consequently, Iles had to give up his directorships – which brought him an annual income of £10,000 alone – and exchange his magnificent clifftop mansion at Dumpton – now Laleham Gap House school in Southcliffe Parade – for a modest bungalow, named Aurora, in Herschell Road, Birchington. He took on a part time job writing for the British Bandsman magazine until his death in 1951. This may seem an odd move at first sight but Iles had in fact been a prominent figure in this country's brass band movement for many years before buying Dreamland. Through his advertising agency he had sponsored numerous major competitions and supported the Bessies O' The Barn in the years prior to the First World War. Iles is remembered to this day by a bench in the village's All Saints churchyard.

His interests were taken over by son Eric and son-in-law Howard Goldby. Within a year Eric was in sole charge. Eric was more cautious than his father and halted further development of Dreamland while making stringent economies. Lewis Gerard, who earned a high salary befitting his status, volunteered to leave as he could – and did – easily find another post. He played himself out in March 1938 and would not return for another nine years.

As war clouds began to gather in 1939, most people were preparing themselves for conflict but many still grabbed the chance for some holiday by the seaside in what was to be a near full length season.

73. Let's hope these youngsters weren't planning to drive very far in the racers when they turned up for Kiddies Day in 1934 – most of them can't see over the steeering wheel! Happily, all have a firm hand on the external handbrake.

Adult and children's parties were still being enticed to Dreamland. A publicity brochure for 'kiddies' states: "We will help you to give the children the happiest time they have ever known." The Scenic Railway is described as 'the securely enthroned monarch of amusement park rides and provides its patrons not only with rib-tickling sensations, but also healthy gulps of fresh air'. No doubt whether they wanted them or not, depending in no small measure on the skills of the brakeman controlling the train from his seat between the first and second cars.

74. Kiddies Day in September 1934 saw a massive Guy Fawkes and bonfire built as centrepiece of a special fireworks display. Children would be given paper fancy dress costumes and free rides.

75. *A view of the park taken in the immediate years prior to World War Two.*

76. *Modernist 1930s styling was followed for the design of the buffet and miniature railway as well as the arcade.*

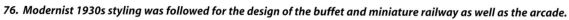

Wild rumours had been circulating about Dreamland's future ever since John Henry's sudden departure the year before but had proved unfounded and the business was intact as war was declared on 3 September 1939. The park closed at once but the cinema and ballroom continued throughout what became known as the phoney war.

One respected figure at Dreamland was lost this year when chief engineer Edmund Mancey, who had been John Henry's right hand man, sadly died.

The cinema and ballroom continued to stay open during the first half of 1940 – two sessions of roller skating were offered on Tuesdays, Thursday and Saturdays. The cinema was showing films such as Jane Withers and the Ritz Brothers in 'We're in the Army Now'.

Meanwhile the management tried to stay optimistic about prospects for the coming summer. Indeed, a mail out to 1,500 previous beano party organisers in the early spring was particularly upbeat about taking bookings, revising menu costs only slightly upwards by around 3d to 4d per head on the previous season.

The letter stated: "At Margate, it will be business as usual and all sections of the town are going full

77. In the 1930s there appeared to be no issue about asking a short man to stand on top of some wooden steps to help instal outdoor lighting. All was well while he could smoke a cigarette while working.

78. Among the wilder rides in the 1930s was the Rocket Planes, variously known as Loop-o-Planes, which were twin cars mounted on a vertical rotating arm giving the feeling of looping or diving. A ride best enjoyed before lunch!

79. The Chaser was one of a number of rides operated by the Studt family as concessionaires in the late 1930s.

out to make the visitor forget the war and to give that jolly good time which only Margate can."

Many outings had already been booked up despite hostilities, the letter said.

"After this winter blackout, killing weather and war work strain, you need relaxation more than ever. Margate and Dreamland will work wonders," it added.

In June the entire site was requisitioned by the Government for a different kind of welcome to Margate. This was the Dunkerque evacuation which saw thousands of troops pour into towns along the East Kent coast.

The restaurants became first aid centres and a procession of stretchers and a seemingly endless stream of walking wounded kept volunteers busy

80. Park view showing the Caterpillar, left, Motor Boats, sideshows and Scenic Railway where a peak capped ride attendant is collecting fares.

Making the dream come true

81. *The Cycle Drome roundabout style ride proved popular in 1938 and was another concession of the Studt family.*

offering what treatment they could. They also wrote hundreds of post cards with the jubilant message 'Safe in England' which were posted to homes all over the country.

Meanwhile the ballroom became a large dormitory. Beds and bedding were brought in and settees, originally used for resting weary dancers now comforted those who had, only hours before, limped off the Dunkerque sand dunes.

A wrinkled old French woman who had trudged miles to reach a boat still clutched her pet dog. Although weary she kept up her spirits frequently shouting 'Vive La France' but her real grief came when she was told her dog had to be taken away and put in quarantine. She wept bitterly.

In happier mood were two Belgian girls who had made their way to Dunkerque and, anxious to reach England, had somehow acquired two soldiers uniforms. One observer noted Dreamland seemed like a fairyland to them. The Garden Café became an interrogation centre for it was always possible that a fifth columnist had been planted among the hundreds of soldiers and civilians being landed in the town.

Although Eric Iles, seeing no prospect of Dreamland being able to trade profitably for the duration, had put the holding company Margate Estates Ltd into voluntary liquidation and laid off the staff including himself, the complex was still active.

The dining halls beneath the cinema were fitted out as decontamination centres, in the event that gas bombs were dropped on the town, bedding and mattresses were stacked up in the ballroom for the Ministry of Supply where camouflage netting was also made. This would then be

dipped in creosote in the buffet building alongside the miniature railway before being hung up to dry under the canopy of the dodgem track.

The coach and car parks were very useful for parking vehicles and storage space.

Dreamland picked up its fair share of scars during the war, fire bombs fell several times near the park boundaries and a long range shell blew away part of the cinema wall. The other local cinemas, the Astoria and Regal, were not so fortunate, both being completely destroyed in different air raids.

Meanwhile, Len Mancey, son of John Henry Iles' right hand man Edmund Mancey, became caretaker manager of Dreamland during this time. He formed his own band to hold dances – nicknamed Mancey's Marathons – in the Garden Café for the Red Cross prisoner of war fund. These events were well attended by soldiers billeted in the town and returning residents – by

82. *Let's hope the engine's boiler wasn't too hot when these young ladies clambered aboard in the 1930s.*

83. In 1937 the Royal Coronation Midgets spent the season at Dreamland and were soon at work building their summer quarters. The public paid to see them go about their daily chores and watch their acrobatic displays.

84. A horse and jockey canter along the beach to race to Dreamland – one of many promotional gimmicks to keep the customers coming.

the time the war was over they had raised £8,000.

It was Len's job, assisted by nightwatchman Jock Ross, to ensure the complex stayed in good order and could be quickly reopened when hostilities ended. In the ballroom and cinema they had to pump large tins of Keating's Powder over the carpets and seats to prevent moth attack. Len serviced the Compton organ – and taught himself to play it too. The building's air conditioning system, motors on rides in the park, including the Scenic Railway, were all regularly serviced.

Len had joined the company in 1937 as a stores clerk at his father's invitation and moved with his wife to Waverley Road, Westbrook. After the Second World War, Len was given control of the park and the indoor skating rink. He stayed with Dreamland until retirement in 1965 and eventually died in 1979, aged 80.

Hostilities in Europe ended on 8 May 1945 and work began soon after to get the park, the cinema and the ballroom open for public use.

The good times would soon be back.

Making the dream come true

85. It's ladies only for this shot of the Brooklands Racers in the late 1940s as Dreamland got into its stride after WW2.

Post war revival

This was the era of demob suits and gratuities, with fun starved families flocking to the seaside for the first time in years to recover from the pressures of war and escape, albeit briefly, from a world still bogged down by rationing. According to the Isle of Thanet Gazette, during one of the first weekends that special trains had started running to Margate more than 20,000 people had visited the town.

In short, there were plenty of people determined to have some fun.

After several months work and negotiating around licences for building materials, the park reopened in June 1946. Although it appeared sparse, the few hastily prepared stalls and rides were an unqualified success – a sign of great prosperity to follow. Workmen toiled hard at night to bring more rides back in to use week by week.

The cinema reopened on 1 July showing the musical comedy Meet The Navy and the ballroom welcomed dancers back on 13 July with 'a special engagement of Roy Richards and his famous ballroom orchestra'.

86. Kelly's Wedding was one of the many sideshows to be found as the park reopened after World War Two.

87. The Dreamland staff assemble for a group photo in front of the cinema entrance in 1946. Gregory Peck was starring in that week's film Spellbound. Dancing in the great ballroom was to the Thanet Strict Tempo Dance Band.

Eric Iles resumed his managerial mantle of Margate Estates. He never liked the idea of being considered a showman and was at pains to point out he was in fact an administrator. His strength of purpose and strong will enabled him to start

88. Eric Iles, who put Dreamland back on its feet after WW2 and continued at the helm until the early 1970s.

Dreamland all over again and consolidate the business.

Showman or not, Eric was keenly perceptive about entertainment. His interest in finding new rides was unending. When trying out a ride on business trips to parks abroad, he would pass his hat and briefcase to wife Doris, carefully time it, note how long it took to load, unload and how many customers boarded.

He would take a camera to picture lighting effects or novelties which might be brought to Dreamland.

Holiday camp king Billy Butlin was appointed Chairman of Margate Estates in 1947 and invested £160,000 in the company – around £6 million in today's money – to get Dreamland fully back on its feet. His investment was a wise one for the company made a record profit of £104,000 that year, again equivalent to several millions today, declaring a shareholders' dividend of 17 per cent.

Butlin had great influence on post war Margate, operating a number of hotels at Cliftonville and, it is said, at one point during this austerity era was even tipped to become Mayor or honorary Alderman of the borough.

Butlin's wide contacts proved very useful in finding new attractions for production of fairground equipment which – like everything else – was in short supply. One ride he secured

89. Coach parties were big business and there were at least 50 vehicles here on this summer's day in the early 1950s.

for the park, though not new, was a treasured Galloping Horses roundabout. When it arrived in Margate in 1946, this 19th century steam powered antiquity came complete with a French organ to supply the music. This later deteriorated and replacement parts could no longer be obtained so it was converted to electricity.

The post war public revelled in sideshows such as Tip The Lady Out of Bed in which, as the name suggests, punters were invited to cast a suitably scantily clad girl into a bath of water when a ball scored a direct hit on a tilt lever. Another woman was encased in ice while elsewhere dark skinned men played voodoo drums.

90. Photographed in 1951, this is thought to be the steam driven Galloping Horses roundabout introduced by Billy Butlin just after World War Two. Conversion to electricity ensured it remained a mainstay of the park for many years.

91. Crowds throng the sideshows in 1950, taking the chance to get away from austerity for a few hours.

Dwarves, under the management of Alan Gale who later went on to promote other shows in Margate, had returned to Dreamland and had set up quarters in the number five hall near the park entrance. Often these people of restricted height would build their own home for the summer season and go about their daily chores as the paying public watched.

Thursday night was fireworks night. Displays once again became a summer attraction. They appealed to adults, who had seen nothing like them since pre-war days, as well as children who had never seen fireworks. Large crowds gathered every week to see the dazzling displays of Brock's fireworks. Although these extravaganzas lasted 20 minutes, it took Dreamland's staff three days to set them up.

Many of the publicity pictures in these immediate post war years had changed little since before 1939 for the simple reason the park hadn't changed a great deal – all of its key attractions like the Caterpillar, the Scenic Railway, the Tubs and the Racing Coaster were still firm favourites with the masses.

Prices had changed though. Lunch menus for beano parties were now five shillings (25p) per head but you were still offered soup, plaice and chips or roast beef and Yorkshire pudding with vegetables and, for dessert, fruit pudding and custard with a cup of tea or coffee.

Out of season, a busy programme of events was put together for the Christmas and New Year period and included being able to see the Walt Disney's Bambi or Danny Kaye in Up In Arms in the cinema. The ballroom offered dancing on Christmas Eve from 8pm to 11.45pm, admission 3/6d, and a New Year's Eve Ball on 31 December from 8pm to 1am, admission five shillings (25p). The Sunshine Café was open daily, except Sundays for darts, billiards and table tennis and the Popular Restaurant hosted three indoor bowling rinks.

Skaters could enjoy the second annual half mile Invicta speed race where the first prize was a pair of new skates worth six guineas (£6.30). An exhibition of free style skating was to be given by NSA gold medallist June Mount on 29 December 1948.

A major setback to this renewed popularity came in August 1949 when the Scenic Railway caught fire, destroying at least half the structure.

The alarm was raised by 21 year old Yvonne Longhi, of nearby Marine Terrace, who woke up to see flames underneath the ride. As she was phoning the fire brigade, so the flames shot up to 50 feet. The brigade sent all nearby machines in Thanet and were joined by more from RAF Manston. The firemen had to break through locked main gates and quickly drained the boating pool before controlling the blaze.

With gas cylinders exploding and the flames working their way towards the zoo, a vet stood by ready to shoot the animals – a lioness, a bear, baboons and a baby monkey among them. Happily, he wasn't needed as the fire was contained in time.

The aftermath of the blaze left the management with a major problem. Wood was still a restricted material and in great demand for rebuilding bomb damaged homes and supplies were scarce. Managers resigned themselves to taking some years to completing repair work.

92. *Standing up in the Scenic Railway cars has always been forbidden – but there's always one who tries.*

93. *A fifties view of the Scenic Railway. Note the large greenhouses in the void space for growing geraniums.*

94. Pony rides in the park, and behind, the Peter Pan railway offered sedate pleasures for younger children.

The solution to the problem came in a most unlikely fashion. Eric Iles and chief engineer Jack Lynch, who had joined in 1946, were flying back from Denmark after viewing potential new rides in the Tivoli Gardens when somebody noticed below the sorry war damaged remains of Lowestoft Pier. The timber would be just what was needed for the Scenic Railway and enquiries about buying the wood were made almost immediately after the plane touched down. It transpired that a Portsmouth firm had already bought it but agreed to sell, with official blessing, some 30,000 cubic feet – or 180 standards – of Lowestoft Pier.

The pier was rebuilt in concrete and stands to this day. The timber eventually arrived in Margate but one job which had to be undertaken first was removal of hundreds of 10 inch nails buried deep in the wood. For years these had held the old pier together against the ravages of the North Sea.

Incidentally, the rides viewed in Denmark's national aquarium were never followed up as there were insurmountable difficulties in constantly pumping the water involved. Ultimately, the trip proved worthwhile as the Scenic Railway was rebuilt in time for the following season.

95. Workmen carry out essential maintenance to steam loco Prince Edward of Wales sometime in the 1950s .

96. Steam loco Billie simmers at the beginning of another day on the Miniature Railway in 1948.

97. Billie again in 1949. By now it had acquired smoke deflectors and a new livery.

98. Slightly obscured by a lamppost, Prince Edward of Wales, nearest camera, joins Billie.

99. was one of the Magic Garden's highlights when opened in 1951.

100. No garden was complete without its gnomes. Dreamland had an entire colony – and saucer eyed trees too.

In spite of pleas from the town's hotels and Dreamland, Margate Council would not follow the current trend of providing night time illuminations. Many resorts, including nearby rival Ramsgate, had realised this brought valuable trade to their towns.

Eric Iles decided he had to do something about this deficiency. He tasked his engineering team, led by Jack Lynch, to install £10,000 worth of decorative lighting and illuminated figures in the ornamental gardens, still attractive with the old Sanger statues, and call it The Magic Garden.

It took only two months to complete the job. Electricians and workmen erected scores of enchanting and ingenious displays based on nursery rhymes, classical mythology, the circus and the jungle. There were electric snowdrops and daffodils and an Orange Grove with specially blown lamps shaped like the fruit.

The opening of the Magic Garden on 5 August 1950 caused a sensation – in the first six evenings 15,000 people queued to view it, paying one shilling (5p) each.

One of the garden's most delightful features, a detailed miniature Tudor village, was transferred in 1953 to become an attraction in its own right on Ramsgate's West Cliff. The Model Village

101. A fairytale character riding a magic swan added to the garden's glory.

celebrated its 50th anniversary in June 2003. Sadly, little more than a month later owner Ken Wake announced closure in September owing to vandalism and falling visitor numbers.

Within months the cliff top site had been levelled and any sign of the Model Village was gone forever. Luckily, a number of its buildings were removed to Salmestone Grange, Margate, by the end of 2003 but some were lost altogether as they could not be lifted.

102. Larger than life multi-coloured butterflies, water lilies and an ornamental magical bridge added to the charm.

If the Scenic Railway fire in 1949 had been a setback, worse was to follow. One night in August 1950 holidaymakers thronged the streets, some in their nightwear, as a huge blaze destroyed the large arcade. Within minutes flames were shooting 100 feet high and the sound of small explosions rent the air. These were asbestos roof panels disintegrating in the heat. Houses in two nearby roads were evacuated by firemen who had been despatched from all over East Kent to quench the flames.

It was reckoned by the end that £75,000 worth of damage had been done – all at the peak of one of Dreamland's most prosperous seasons. In today's money that's more than £2 million.

Loyal staff, some returning off duty, did all they could to help but about 20 stalls were gutted and others severely damaged. A local paper report noted that in the centre of the arcade a soft drink stall remained completely untouched by the fire.

The arcade had lasted barely 20 years, replacing one of the former hangars JH Iles had built soon after taking over the park.

103. *This photo of the Octopus Ride, centre, was taken just days before the arcade, top, burnt down in 1950.*

104. *Some of the tangled remains of the arcade after the great fire of 1950.*

105. A view of the Swiss Beer Garden which was added to the Magic Garden in 1951.

On 1 June 1951, the Isle of Thanet Gazette announced the death of John Henry Iles. Funfair king, musician, champion of working men's brass bands and journalist, he was 79 years old. Since his bankruptcy in 1938 he had lived in Birchington. His funeral at the village's All Saints' church, was conducted by Rev NM Grenville Sharp. A large congregation was entertained by the village silver band and organist Lewis Gerard, who had returned to Dreamland a few years earlier. The church was lined with more than 80 floral tributes.

At this time an uneasy peace had arrived between the council and Dreamland over the lack of illuminations such that the Mayor was invited to officially open the Magic Garden for the 1951 summer season.

With the additions this year of a Swiss Beer Garden and a mechanical Oompah band playing from a Tyrolean bandstand, it was one of Dreamland's most charming aspects. Not only did the half life size figures play instruments, but their heads nodded, feet tapped and eyes rolled in time to recorded music.

106. It's plain to see how immaculately well kept the gardens were in this daytime view from the early 1950s.

107. *The 330 feet replica of the Queen Mary takes centre stage in this view of the park, taken from the Scenic Railway in August 1953. London Transport double deckers stand out in the coach park while, nearby, roller skaters get their balance.*

1951 is best remembered for the Festival of Britain with a major exhibition of all the latest British innovations on London's South Bank. Dreamland's electricians and engineers were seconded to the site to help build the fairground and it was while the work was going on that Eric Iles met young designer Ross Grundy. Between them they came up with the design for the replica Queen Mary to stand along one side of the amusement park until the late 1970s.

Set at one end of the coach park the new structure had to have an interesting outline. It would be solid on its seaward side while housing a line of stalls on the side facing into the park. Despite suffering fire itself in September 1963, the 330 feet long Queen Mary dominated the amusement park scene for the next 26 years.

The original refusal of Margate Council to give it permanent planning permission influenced its somewhat flimsy construction which meant that by 1977 it had deteriorated beyond repair and had to be demolished.

Small round cabins 15 feet deep by 25 feet in diameter were built into two of the Queen Mary's funnels. One was like a small broadcasting studio from where operator Stan Sawyer would give commentaries over the public address system for the weekly firework displays and it was his playing of the record When Day is Done that signalled the nightly closure of the park.

The other was used as a look out post from where supervisors could keep an eye on the park and the staff. One of their tasks was called spotting. Aided by a blackboard and binoculars they would attempt to record the number of customers boarding a particular ride over a given period, later to be matched – or otherwise – with the cashier's takings, in an effort to deter, if not detect, any dishonest practices!

108. *A line of sideshows was housed along one side of the Queen Mary replica and were proving busy in July 1952.*

Post war revival

All of the pictures on this page show members of the Studt family and their sideshows in 1953.
109. Above: Well turned out family members gather for a group photo on the Spinner sideshow.
110. Top right: The Bingo booth offered an array of prizes for lucky winners in the days before gambling laws changed, paving the way for large bingo halls.
111. Centre right: Exterior view of the Bingo booth with the Scenic Railway beyond.
112. Bottom: The Studt family had the concession for the Winchester Rifle Range for many years.

Speaking on his appointment as company chairman in July 1969, Eric Iles said he got the idea for the Queen Mary replica while travelling on the real liner to the USA during one of his trips to explore new rides abroad.

"It gave me the idea for reproducing the familiar lines of the craft as the outstanding feature of the park. The idea crystallised completely during my return trip on the Queen Elizabeth," he said.

Rebuilding the Scenic Railway a couple of years earlier had enabled one of the high runs to be extended. Around this time was built underneath it the Canonbury near-beer bar, which tended to be patronised by those who wanted to continue drinking after the real beer bars had closed, before sleeping it all off in the gardens. Later on it became a cafeteria. Next to this was what became the Scenic Theatre. To the accompaniment of frequent roars of the scenic's cars passing overhead, a succession of bizarre shows was presented. The semi-static Dracula's Daughter, the Headless Lady and the Living Half-Lady, made and owned by one time fire eater Jon Gresham, appeared here along with illusionist Al Davis and his wife with their mentalists' act – The Amazing Margoes and showman illusionist Knox-Crichton whose wife was The Floating Lady.

113. Judging by their skilful technique and smart skating boots, the two girls on the left were regular visitors to the roller rink in 1954. Compare them with the others who are less steady on their feet!

Roller skating enjoyed a resurgence after 1945, with competitions and gala nights for speed skating and roller dance skating. Rink hockey matches saw teams like the Dreamlandiers or Ramsgate Redwings competing against visiting teams from as far as Dartford, Brixton, Cricklewood, Southend – even Paris.

Skating, both indoors and outdoors, had been a popular activity ever since the Hall By The Sea became fully established and tuition was readily available for novices and those wanting to enjoy it more seriously. By the 1960s though, changing tastes saw skating disappear and it would not return until making a brief comeback in 1980.

114. Roller hockey teams Margate Shamrocks and Ramsgate Redwings, in quartered shirts, pose after a big game in 1951.

Post war revival

115. The Whirlwind Racer ride in 1954. People still looked formally dressed for a day by the sea.

With competition increasing from other seaside resorts, Dreamland was having to work harder to bring people to Margate and by 1950 it had developed a holiday package. Hotels and boarding houses in Margate, Cliftonville, Westgate and Westbrook were able to offer their guests The Key To Freedom.

This enabled holidaymakers to have a free pass for the duration of their stay for dancing in Dreamland's ballroom, cinema, fireworks displays and enjoy rides on the Scenic Railway. It also gave them the best seats at the Lido Theatre and go greyhound racing at Dumpton track, on the edge of Ramsgate – both sister operations of Margate Estates.

A colourful publicity leaflet assured guests they would have 'the same welcome and privileges as if you were putting your money down'. Unlimited visits and use were included with weekly hotel charges.

It went on to say: "Ask yourself if this is not a grand offer. It is an honest endeavour by hoteliers to give the holiday public something in keeping with the times. The wonderful advantage is that you know the cost of your holiday in advance and we are confident that when you compare the charges with hotels not offering freedom holidays you will agree it is the most attractive value ever placed before the holiday maker."

With a Freedom Holiday you are freed from the constant drain upon your purse, it added.

By 1952, the Dreamland kitchens in the height of summer were serving 3,000 meals a day for the beanfeast parties still coming to the park. A catering staff of 200 worked the eight restaurants and four kitchens. During the season some 70,000 were catered for. Not as impressive as figures for 20 years earlier but still making a profit.

116. The Peter Pan railway was a perennial favourite for younger visitors to the park when this view was captured in 1954.

117. Rumbustious goings on were the hallmark of Old Time Music Hall in the Sunshine Theatre from the mid 1950s.

The same year saw the Sunshine Café converted to the Old Time Music Hall with Bill Bennett-Hamley, Dreamland's entertainment manager, as chairman, going under the name of Mr Thanet Friendly. There were queues at the door every evening and it was warmly received by locals as well as visitors. The café's stylish decorations, including a distinctive Art Deco mural by Walpole Champneys, were, controversially now, replaced by opulent

118. A sketch set in the parlour of the Sea View Boarding House, 1895, was all part of the Old Time fare.

Edwardian effects for an authentic atmosphere. The audience, seated at tables in the authentic manner, were entertained to a rumbustious show – at h'enormous h'expense of course.

The portly and bewhiskered Ted Gatty took over as chairman a year or two later and in 1960 became responsible for running the whole show after Alan Gale was unable to agree new terms. Ted ran Old Time Music Hall for a further seven seasons.

This all started a new attraction for families who wanted to spend a merry evening with hard and soft drinks within reach and was a hint of the club style show which would change national entertainment tastes.

By 1956 Old Time Music Hall in the Sunshine Theatre during the summer months was becoming firmly established with five changes of billing each week – a slightly different show, with a different printed programme each night of the week aimed at capturing guests from local guest houses and hotels. By now the chairman was Ted Gatty, who lived in Broadstairs, but Alan Gale would continue as producer until 1959 when he was unable to agree new terms with Eric Iles. The original idea for Old Time Musical Hall in this format had come from another production at Battersea in 1951, further developed by Alan and paved the way for BBC TVs Good Old Days programme of the later 1950s and 1960s. Names on the Dreamland bill included such entertainers as soprano Patricia Kay and comedian Freddy Liston.

121. Teddy Boys were making their presence known – and sometimes felt – in the park by 1954.

119. Holding on tight are a couple of apprehensive customers on the Whip ride in August 1954.

120. Professional roller skating displays were a feature on the rink in the Garden Café during the post war era.

122. The Climbing Monkeys sideshow, seen here in 1956, saw players aiming to be first to get the toy monkey to the top of the pole.

123. Road rage on the Brooklands Racers – surely not! Look closely at this 1954 image for the two girls having a finger pointed at them for some minor misdemeanour.

CORONATION CELEBRATIONS AT DREAMLAND

THREE GLORIOUS DAYS

SATURDAY, 30th MAY

BALLROOM 7.30 p.m.—11.45 p.m. Admn. 4/-
GREAT FESTIVE GALA
FUN, GAMES, HATS, BALLOONS & PRIZES — ALAN GREEN & HIS BAND

AMUSEMENT PARK At Dusk. Admission to Park 1/-, Children 6d.
MAGNIFICENT DISPLAY OF BROCKS'
REGAL FIREWORKS
ALSO
PATRIOTIC SING-SONG ON ARENA GRANDSTAND--Seats 6d.

MONDAY, 1st JUNE

CINEMA

Mon., Tues., & Wed.	Thurs., Fri., & Sat.
RICHARD WIDMARK in **DESTINATION GOBI** (U) and Susan Hayward & Charlton Heston in **THE PRESIDENT'S LADY** (A)	Robert Mitchum & Susan Hayward in **THE LUSTY MEN** (U) and **KON-TIKI** (U)

BALLROOM 7.30—11 p.m. Admission 3/6
A CELEBRATION REVEL
SPECIAL JOLLITY NIGHT, HATS AND BALLOONS WITH ALAN GREEN

AMUSEMENT PARK CAR PARK ARENA, 6.45 p.m.
ADMISSION TO PARK FREE
A GREAT PATRIOTIC DEMONSTRATION AND DISPLAY
FESTIVAL OF SERVICE
MARGATE TOWNSPEOPLE OFFER THEIR TRIBUTE TO THE COUNTRY
DISPLAYS AND DEMONSTRATIONS by Civil Defence, W.V.S., Sea Cadets, 438 Sqd. A.T.C., Women's Junior Air Corps 1580 (Thanet) Unit, St. John Ambulance, (Westgate and Birchington), Council of Ex-Servicemen, School Children from St. Gregory's and Draper's Mills Schools
ALSO **GRAND PARADE OF LOYALTY** including
The Old Contemptibles Association, British Legion, Royal Naval Association, Association of Jewish Ex-Servicemen and Women, Royal Artillery Association, Past and Present Buffs, R.A.F. Association, Royal National Life Boat Institution, Margate Ambulance Corps, Margate Girl Guides, Margate Sea Rangers, British Red Cross Society (Thanet Branch), and the Association of WRENS.
Admission to Arena (6,000 Seats): Centre Block 1/6, Child 9d.; Other Seats 1/-, Child 6d.; Standing 9d., Child 6d. No charge to view C.D. Display

TUES. CORONATION DAY 2nd JUNE

SUNSHINE CAFE 10 a.m.—5 p.m. (Continuous)
LARGE SCREEN TELEVISION
ALSO A BATTERY OF STANDARD SIZE T.V. SETS
SO ALL MAY SEE CEREMONY AND PROCESSION
LICENSED AND OTHER REFRESHMENTS AT POPULAR PRICES
NO CHARGE TO VIEW REFRESHMENT TICKETS 6d.

AMUSEMENT PARK ADMISSION FREE
GREAT OUTDOOR CARNIVAL
FREE RIDES GIVEN TO ALL IN HOME-MADE FANCY DRESS & ORIGINAL "GET-UP"
1,000's OF FREE RIDES - TREASURE HUNT CARNIVAL HATS GIVEN FREE
ROASTING THE OX WHOLE
From 2 p.m.—SIGHT OF A LIFETIME—DISTRIBUTION OF MEAT.
CARVING CEREMONY, FIRST CUT BY HIS WORSHIP THE MAYOR
(Alderman H. V. WARD, J.P.)
ALSO **GIANT BONFIRE**

BALLROOM 7.30 p.m.—1 a.m. Admission 4/-
THE CORONATION BALL
SUNSHINE & SMILES CABARET
ROASTED OX—Meat Undistributed in Park GIVEN AWAY FREE
Hats, Balloons, Prizes & Alan Green's Band. A Super Fun Night

SUNDAY, 7th JUNE

COACH PARK ARENA 10.45 a.m. Admission Free
MASSED THANKSGIVING SERVICE
(Interdenominational)
Organised by the Vicar of Margate, (The Rev. Sydney A. Odom)

VM/35511/F.P.C.

The Queen's Coronation in June 1953 saw special celebrations at Dreamland which actually began on Saturday 30 May with a festive gala in the ballroom and a firework display with patriotic sing song in the park. Admission to the ball was four shillings a head and a seat at the fireworks was sixpence.

The following Monday a Festival of Service had been arranged where 'Margate townspeople offer their tribute to the country'.

Demonstrations were given by Civil Defence units, St John Ambulance and WRVS. Local schools rubbed shoulders with war veterans, Girl Guides, the RNLI and the Royal British Legion for the occasion which also included a 'grand parade of loyalty'.

Coronation Day itself, Tuesday 2 June, brought the chance for people to view the Westminster service itself on a large screen TV in the Sunshine Café. A battery of standard sized TVs was also provided. There was no charge to view but the bar was open and refreshment tickets cost 6d each. Exactly how big a large screen TV would have been is open to interpretation but it's worth remembering the Coronation provided the impetus for many people in Britain to buy or rent their first telly – black and white of course – which would have had a screen of little more than nine or 10 inches.

Naturally enough, a Coronation ball was held that evening with dancing to the Alan Green Band and the Sunshine and Smiles cabaret. Admission was four shillings (20p).

In the park, the queen's crowning saw dozens of people turn out in fancy dress to be given free rides for the day and take part in a treasure hunt. A whole ox was roasted on a spit with the first cut made by the town mayor, Alderman Harry Ward.

The celebrations were rounded off on the following Sunday with an interdenominational massed thanksgiving service in the coach park arena, organised by the vicar of Margate Rev Sydney Odom.

A new ride this year was the Skywheels ride. Built by the park's skilled engineers, it became a particular favourite with USAF airmen based at Manston. Its twin wheels rotated independently and turned one over the other. Definitely a ride to enjoy before lunch, not after.

124. How Dreamland celebrated the Queen's Coronation in 1953. Was the massed thanksgiving service in the coach park a success?

One Dreamland custom which disappeared around this time was Mother's Day. For years this was a Monday when merry parties of East End women invaded Dreamland and brought the cockney spirit to the park. Typical of these jovial jaunts was the woman – predictably there was a different one each week – who wore bloomers emblazoned with the Union Jack and cheerfully bent over to display them to passers by. Accompanied, of course, by hearty guffaws of laughter from her friends.

A number of sideshows were organised this time by Alan Gale and included Miranda – Margate's Modern Mermaid – actually four girls who took turns to lay submerged in a tank of water, breathing through a carefully concealed air tube; Katrina, a clairvoyant, and The Madcap Family – mechanical figures from France whose progress on a cycling holiday was shown in a series of amusing dioramas.

125. The mind boggles at the apparent absence of safety rails as the crowd gathers to watch a motorbike stuntman go through his paces outside the Wall of Death.

126. A 1950s poster persuading outing parties to come to Margate.

Not far away was The Scenic Theatre. In it, to the accompaniment of frequent roars from the Scenic Railway trains passing overhead, a succession of bizarre shows was presented. They ranged from the semi-static Dracula's Daughter, Headless Lady and Living Half Lady, made and owned by one time magician and fire eater Jon Gresham, to short performances by well known illusionists like Al Davis and his wife with their mentalists' act, The Amazing Margoes, in 1955, and showman illusionist Knox-Crichton whose wife was The Floating Lady.

Dreamland park long had story value for the local and national newspapers. Even a power failure in the fifties somehow became more agreeable the next day when readers learned the River Caves had provided a useful side effect.

'A dream came true last night for couples in love... they were in Dreamland's Tunnel of Love and there was a power failure', announced a Sunday paper.

It went on to say the courting couples were isolated 'for 10 whole minutes', adding that stallholders had to wade through the water to push them into the open. It doesn't say what sort of reception they got!

127. After the Queen Mary replica was installed in 1953, the Brookland Racers circuit was relocated more to the centre of the main park. Previously, it had been on a lower level withthe main car park.

Dreamland's technical staff had been hard at work during the early part of 1954 building a new giant screen in the cinema. Measuring 38 feet by 45 feet, it virtually filled the proscenium arch. By Easter in April, the week's programme included the newly released Doctor In The House film starring Dirk Bogarde, Kenneth More and Donald Sinden. Television was becoming more popular and the decades old habit for most people to go to the pictures once or twice a week was on the wane.

128. The Ovaltiney Puppet Show came to the Sunshine Theatre in the early 1950s – and proved a big hit with young fans of the radio show.

For younger customers, the Dreamland Minors Club met for Saturday morning cinema promptly at 10am. Christmas Eve 1954 promised a special show with dancing on the stage and Uncle Ben playing favourite carols. New Year holiday billing included good old fashioned cowboys and indians films but the newly released White Christmas with Bing Crosby, Danny Kaye and Rosemary Clooney was a highlight, especially as it was to be screened in VistaVision for greater clarity.

The growing influence of television coverage was fully felt by Dreamland when BBC's Panorama programme showed excerpts of a short film by independent maker Lindsay Anderson entitled 'O Dreamland' in 1956.

Although made three years earlier, the 12 minute production had been shelved but won national publicity when it was in line for an award. O Dreamland showed an allegedly darker side of the park, featuring bleak and unattractive photography with a soundtrack highlighting the laughter of mechanical puppets.

The film clearly conveys Anderson's critical view of Dreamland's attractions – a Torture through the Ages exhibit; bingo; penny arcades; bangers, beans and chips and seemingly endless puppets.

As if this wasn't bad enough, Panorama's distinguished presenter Richard Dimbleby said after the piece had been screened that if he went

129. *The beach scene on a typically warm August Bank Holiday in the mid 1950s – then at the beginning of the month.*

to Margate, he would see his children didn't go to Dreamland.

Understandably, Eric Iles was furious at the park being shown in the wrong light and briefly considered legal action but eventually backed down. O Dreamland was made after Anderson had completed making a short documentary Thursday's Children, about life at Margate's Royal School for Deaf Children, which eventually won an Oscar.

1958 was the year Dreamland bade farewell to the Americans based at Manston, who had been loyal and regular customers to the cinema, ballroom and park throughout their posting in this country. A ceremony was held in the Sunshine Café in April during which a painting of Dreamland was presented to 406 squadron before the venue was reset for that summer's Old Time Music Hall.

Once the season had ended, the building was redecorated and reopened on Saturday 1 November with advertisements proclaiming two ballrooms and two bands – in reality the Sunshine Café had become the second smaller dancing arena – while the bands were Noel Davis and His Music and George Dunn and His Modernaires.

In 1960 the cinema's crop of Biblical epics in the late fifties no doubt inspired the real life impersonation of Sampson, a strongman, with Delilah, in 1958. Laurie Stagg, retiring from

130. *Park staff, including some who worked in the offices, pose at the base of the helter skelter in the 1950s.*

131. *The mini coach, based on a Leyland Tiger, usually ferried children between the car and amusement parks but in 1954 comedian Bunny Baron and dancers Betty Lincoln, left, and Joy Martell – two of the Six Eleanor Beams Girls – boarded it for a photocall promoting the Cliftonville Lido's Sunshine and Smiles summer show. The vehicle, powered by an Austin Seven engine, was among 63 built in Brighton between 1935 and 1959 by former bus driver Ernest Johnstone.*

that great speciality act of the variety era, The Australian Air Aces, showed two illusions in the mid sixties, The Amazing Ray and Petra which was a living, talking, smiling disembodied head – both the work of Robert Harbin.

Dancing in the ballroom was still drawing the crowds. Until late June, it was open on Thursday and Saturday nights. From then on until early September, dancing to Ray Gordon and his orchestra could be enjoyed nightly except Sundays and every night was a gift night with prizes to be won including perms, channel cruises and even air trips. Among the sponsors were Babycham, Kleenex Tissues, Brylcreem and Van Houten's chocolate.

Getting the beanfeast parties to Dreamland was still important although perhaps the emphasis had shifted slightly as car ownership was becoming more common. For those without motors, a special version of the illustrated fold out leaflet – it was no longer a booklet – was printed for British Railways Southern Region. Reduced rail fares were available for groups of eight or more, as prior to the Second World War, while for larger parties special trains could be arranged with even lower fares for 30 or more people, particularly if travelling on a weekday. By now hot lunches started at 6/6d (33p) and rose up to 11/6d (57p) while afternoon teas could be had for between three shillings (15p)

and 6/6d (33p). As was usual a slip of paper was enclosed detailing letters from delighted customers. A party of 425 staff from London's Connaught Rooms were among them, saying the meals provided were 'excellent'. Praise indeed.

132. *For the princely sum of 6d, children could ride the mini coach from the car park to a scaled down bus terminal in the park. Of the 17 mini coaches thought to survive, two are kept at the CM Booth Motor Museum, Rolvenden, Kent.*

133. *This mid to late 1950s aerial view may have been taken on a quieter day judging by the handful of coaches parked up. The main sands appear to be filing up with people.*

Built at one end of the Scenic Railway was Zooland, which contained a Monkey Jungle with a large cage filled with more than 40 monkeys scampering over the heads of the public passing through a mesh tunnel. This faced a horseshoe shaped range of conventional cages accommodating lions, bears, foxes, squirrels, pheasants, parrots and owls. A sudden shower of rain would attract a rush of customers to the show. When this happened Arthur Bean who ran Zooland would exhort passers by to "Come inside and see the animals under cover...see the monkeys in the dry."

Anyone who complained the zoo was open to the sky was reproved with the information the

134. *Sharpshooters get their eye in on the Winchester Rifle Range. Operated by the Studt family, its day to day running was, perhaps appropriately, handed to the brother who became permanently deaf after contracting glandular fever as a teenager.*

cages were roofed – no one had suggested the public would not get wet!

Nearby, 'Professor' Tomlin presented his flea circus. It is said his actors were sent to Margate by post from a laboratory. On one occasion, the container was damaged en route and once opened in the Dreamland offices the fleas quickly hopped out and disappeared. During the next few days everyone working there was bitten at least once!

In the 1960s two responses were made in attempts to meet changing tastes in leisure pursuits. Bingo opened in the Sunshine Theatre in November 1963 with a promise of joining in the National Lucky Scoop, a weekly accumulator and a break the bank Snowball. Considered a passing fad which would merely generate some additional revenue in the off season, it grew so much that it became increasingly difficult to justify suspension each summer for the Old Time Music Hall, which it eventually replaced in 1969.

In the ballroom, resident dance bands gave way to single night performers. This policy of occasional engagements developed in the 1950s and saw such bands and groups as those of Ted Heath, Eric Delaney, John Barry and Ray Ellington performing here. The idea became so popular it paved the way to appearances by all the best known bands of the time.

The last of the resident dance bands, Tommy Martin's, played out on 8 September 1962. Several hundred successful weekend appearances by Gerry and the Pacemakers, Freddie and the Dreamers, Brian Poole, Mike Berry, Carl Denver,

135. The rock and roll house made its Dreamland debut in 1958.

136. Dreamland's opulent ballroom was still drawing fair sized gatherings in the fifties.

The Springfields and The Shadows followed.

The Beatles did not appear, but the Rolling Stones did – on 15 August 1963. Remarkably, Mick Jagger and Co weren't top of the bill but were supporting the Barron Knights. The Stones were keenly followed though and had to tough it out in the gents toilets after their performance when the key to their dressing room was lost. Screaming girl fans waited outside!

For many youngsters Sunday evenings was the highlight of the week in the 1960s when the Rendezvous Club would meet in Dreamland's Sunshine Hall. Its rapid success soon saw it transferred to the ballroom. Attendances averaged around 1,000 and groups as well as discos entertained the teenagers. Regular acts included Tommy Martin and His Rebels, Brian Bentley and His All Stars, Grant Tracey and The Sunsets and Frank Kelly and The Hunters.

Others on the bill included Dave Dee, Dozy, Beaky, Mick and Tich, The Knives and Forks, The Crickets, The Plus Four, The Fortunes and the chart topping The Marmalade.

Spinning the discs was a young Mick Tomlinson – better known as Mick Tee – who took over the disco side in 1968. In one capacity or another, he was involved in Dreamland for many years with roles as wide ranging as electrician and advertising manager.

Members of the Rendezvous Club, which celebrated its fiftieth anniversary in 2009, had to be at least 16 years old and a managing committee of five boys and five girls ensured things ran smoothly.

The early and mid 1960s saw greater social changes and these started to have an effect on the Dreamland empire. Mods and rockers regularly converged on Margate at weekends often ending in violent drink fuelled clashes in the park, the seafront or on the nearby beach.

137. A ballroom poster of 1957 promised entertainment six nights a week.

138. Inside the Polynesian themed Bali Hai bar which opened on the seafront in 1967. A flashpoint for many brawls!

Their antics made national headlines in 1963 after an infamous pitched battle on the beach with local police. The town's magistrates dealt severely with the offenders, one JP labelling them 'Sawdust Caesars', a term that stuck and survives in mod sub-culture today.

Holidays by the British seaside fell from favour as large numbers of people opted for the now widely available – and comparatively cheaper – package holidays.

For many years after the war Dreamland cinema, like all others, competed with television to hold audiences. Despite bigger screens and more colour movies it was a losing battle.

However, no change was to be as far reaching as the sale of Margate Estates in July 1968 to Phonographic Equipment Ltd – later to become Associated Leisure Ltd – which bid £1,400,000, about £17,500,000 in today's money.

The announcement came after two other companies, the Ramsgate based Pleasurama fun park and amusement machine operator Clubman's

139. A go kart track came to the park in the early 1960s – and lads were used in the promotional photos.

Post war revival

140. The racers finally got some new cars to drive. They look like scaled down versions of the Austin Cambridge.

Club, had been bidding against each other over the previous four months for Dreamland.

Phonographic's then managing director Cyril Shack said: "Profits will be used to increase facilities at the park for the benefit of the people in the area.

"We think there is tremendous potential and we are hoping we can really awaken the area. We shall put in the best and latest coin machines.

"We want to make Dreamland the finest amusement park in the south of England."

Nevertheless, no changes were immediately apparent other than a proliferation of amusement machine arcades. A link with the

141. The Satellite Ride was popular for much of the 1960s.

past was broken though with the closure by the end of the decade of the open air Rollerink. When the ballroom replaced Sanger's original rink, roller skating had carried on during the winter only in the Garden Café but its popularity faded in the 1930s.

Iles family control continued, for the time being at any rate, with Eric Iles remaining as Chairman, and 29 year old son John, who had joined in 1961 after National Service, becoming Managing Director.

John was soon on the road looking at new attractions to bring to the park and it was at this time that safari parks were becoming increasingly popular.

It was decided to create one at Dreamland, for £30,000, in the ornamental gardens, where the Magic Garden, no longer a novelty, had long since closed.

Kent and England cricket captain, Colin Cowdrey, performed the opening ceremony on July 25 1969 accompanied by Mayor of Margate Cllr Bill Goodrich and his deputy Cllr Harry Anish. Shown around by John and Eric Iles, they were able to observe history repeating itself – the site was built on Sanger's original pleasure garden and animal collection.

Animals were on view 'in close up as never before' according to the publicity and included three lions, a tiger, pumas and a rare binturong from the Phillipines. Arriving soon after were two elephants, a camel and smaller animals for the pets' corner.

Readers of the Isle of Thanet Gazette's Bimbo Club – the weekly children's page – were asked to come up with names for two penguins. Alas, records don't reveal what the ultimate choices were. A 25 feet long python from Malaya, weighing 182lbs, was intended to be the first reptile for a planned snake farm.

Soon after the opening the monkeys escaped – 13 were recaptured quickly but one baboon resisted all attempts and eventually had to be lured back to his enclosure using drugged food.

The zoo was promoted at carnivals all over Kent with a Noah's Ark style float featuring two cages of lions and an elephant ridden by go-go dancer Jacqui Lawrence. Dan Robinson of Scarborough, who later ran the It's A Knockout competitions in the coach park when fireworks displays ended, operated the zoo with Dick Chipperfield, of circus fame, to stock and staff it. Other operators would follow in the years after.

142. The park looked neat and tidy when this photo was taken at the beginning of a summer's day in the early 1960s.

Post war revival

143. The Paratrooper ride was a long time favourite in the park and is seen here in the early 1960s.

John Iles left Dreamland in 1970 to become General Manager of Battersea Fun Fair. At the end of this year Eric Iles chose to retire. He had been involved almost from the beginning helping run the operation with his father and had taken on much of the day to day control of Dreamland from 1929 before becoming a director in 1938. Half a century of Iles family involvement was at an end. Eric later died in Margate hospital on 12 February 1972, aged 72, after a heart attack at his home, Hamilton Lodge in Bishops Avenue, near North Foreland in Broadstairs.

144. The Sky Wheels dated from 1953 having been built by Dreamland's own engineers and was a mainstay of the rides until the late 1970s.

145. A view of the park taken off season from the newly completed Arlington House flats in 1963. The sign on the side of the main building is in good order.

147. A Morse diesel powered locomotive was added to the miniature railway in the latter part of the 1950s and waits alongside while Billie gets close attention.

146. Ready for the off with a packed train is Billie while Prince Edward is on standby sometime in the early 1960s.

148. This 1960s night scene shows the Sky Wheels and the Jets in the foreground. On the left a children's ride stands empty. Youngsters would have been safely in bed.

149. *Miniature locomotive Billie was given a new boiler in 1968 with this picture taken before the cab had been replaced.*

150. *Left, a rare view of the frontage of the Racing Coaster, probably dating from the mid to late 1960s.*

151. *Below, a typical sixties night scene alongside the Scenic Railway. Note the statuary, dating from the park's early years, still in situ on the left hand side.*

152. The Jets ride, introduced in 1957, was still thriving in the new decimal currency world of 1971.

New brooms herald a new era

The new owners had been saying their aim was to make Dreamland the finest amusement complex in the south of England. In March 1969 Phonographic announced a five year plan to make it one of the most modern parks in the world, willing to spend £500,000 fulfilling that promise.

Already £100,000 had been earmarked for the first phase and some of the improvements would be in place for the beginning of the new season

153. The Alice in Wonderland ride ran close to the Queen Mary replica throughout the early 1970s,

at Whitsun. These included new signage and a facelift to the frontage and entrances to the park.

A theatre restaurant was promised where customers would be able to dine and dance while watching top class cabaret shows until the early hours. The bingo club was to be revitalised and the famous Dreamland tunnel, the entrance off the seafront, was to be modernised. A new leisure centre featuring the latest amusement machines, almost all of them British the announcement pointed out, would also make its debut.

Underneath the Scenic Railway a Kiddies Wonderland was planned alongside an arcade named Treasure Island.

The press release boldly promised: "During the next few years we shall be bringing to Dreamland the world's most modern and up to date amusement equipment. Our aim is to enable the public to enjoy their leisure in surroundings that cannot be bettered anywhere in Britain or abroad."

At the same time the company changed its name to Associated Leisure Entertainments Ltd.

Associated Leisure had courted some controversy three years earlier when it had made a takeover bid for Butlin's. The Daily Mail had claimed some of the company's directors were front men for the Mafia.

New brooms herald a new era

154. A walk in the park in the 1970s – the fashions confirm why this was the decade good taste forgot.

A resulting libel case against the newspaper was lost by Associated Leisure in July 1971 and cost them £100,000 in legal fees, even though the directors were innocent.

Douglas Harrison was appointed Managing Director in autumn 1971 after Eric Iles retirement. Called Doug by all who knew him, he had previously been a member of Dreamland's administrative staff who had joined as a cashier in 1946. He would oversee several radical departures from previous operating practices, as well as supervise almost as many changes as Margate had seen in its now lengthy history.

By the time of the announcement, he and other senior managers had travelled more than 40,000 miles seeking new ideas. They went to Germany, Spain and the United States, where they visited Disneyland and Las Vegas. They also looked at nightclubs and discos in Ostend, Belgium, and Torremolinos in Spain. While preserving the best of the old, the new owners set about their task with relish.

The cinema was rapidly becoming unprofitable, handicapped now by its 2,200 capacity. A few concerts by, among others Roy Orbison and Dorothy Squires, had proved outstandingly successful and this indicated a potential for live entertainment on a scale which had not previously been attempted. Accordingly in February 1973 the cinema closed, reopening at Easter with the circle attractively divided – at a cost of more than £55,000 – into two smaller cinemas each seating 350. In the weeks after the

155. A general view of the Whirl-a-Boats ride in 1970. The boats' unreliability won few friends among the operators.

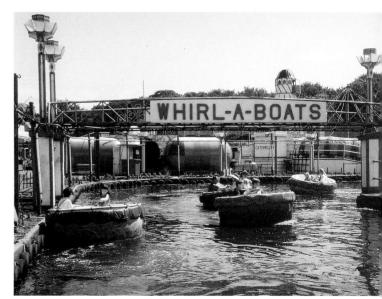

156. A view inside the new look bingo hall after conversion in the 1970s.

opening movie fans were able to choose between seeing The Godfather, Treasure Island, MASH, Butch Cassidy & The Sundance Kid and the new release of James Bond in Live And Let Die.

With echoes of 1935, publicity material announced the new structure had called for 69 tons of timber, 25 tons of steel, 2.5 tons of nails,

157. Market manager Ernest Lea, left with a stallholder in 1978. Note prices for LPs and eight track cartridges!

five tons of acoustic tiles, two tons of floor boards and 20 tons of plaster board!

Seat prices were now 50p and 45p with reductions for children and OAPs. The cost included the newly introduced Value Added Tax.

The former stalls and stage now comprised the Dreamland Theatre where the curtain went up on The Dick Emery Show to a packed house.

Back out in the park new rides were arriving such as 20,000 Leagues Under The Sea. Designed by amusement ride artist Keith Sparks and adapted freely from the Jules Verne tale, it was the first ride of its kind in the country and cost £25,000 to build. By hopping into one of the cars, passengers would be transported to Verne's undersea world, complete with true sound effects and full animation. They would ride through the belly of a whale, past Captain Nemo's machine room, watch an undersea ballet and ride on to groaning ruins of the Lost City of Atlantis to be frightened by hordes of undersea spiders.

The car park had now found another use on Thursdays with a market being held between 9am and 4pm. Although first introduced in December 1971, its path of progress had been a rocky one as planning permission had been refused by the council. Using a special provision which allowed markets to be held on 28 days a year, it had gone ahead anyway proving popular among bargain hunters. A public inquiry was held in January 1973

New brooms herald a new era

158. A scene from the controversial play The Bed while at the Royalty Theatre, London, which featured Jenny Kenna and John Higgins, prior to coming to Dreamland.

and by April it had found in Dreamland's favour. Stallholders were delighted and vowed to make it one of the best on the Kent coast. While there's no certainty about how long the market survived, publicity photos of manager Ernest Lea with stallholders were taken in 1978.

A risqué comedy farce entitled The Bed, presented by Paul Raymond – owner of London's Raymond's Revue Bar and soft porn magazine Men Only – arrived for the summer season and immediately caused controversy.

It's fair to say Margate probably wasn't ready for a play featuring full frontal nudity – residents were suitably shocked and horrified. Despite the attendant publicity, the production which starred John Inman, straight from TVs Are You Being Served, and six female co stars, played to less than full houses.

Dreamland's Funseekers newspaper said: "As the title of the play implies, the farce revolves around a bed, fitted with eccentric gadgetry, which is the proud possession of the central male character who can cause things to happen which give the young ladies in the play plenty to think about."

Naughty but not obscene is how the Isle of Thanet Gazette summed it up: "When one has had an eyeful of bottoms and bosoms it becomes a succession of comic seaside postcards brought to life. All naughty, clean fun without being obscene."

More family oriented entertainment was to be found in the Garden Café where trumpeter Ken Grieff and his trio held sway for a 10 week season until September.

In a June 1973 Dreamland press release Ken correctly observed there was quite a contrast in the kind of entertainment he offered from The Bed. "My audience is largely parents who bring their children for a night's music and sing song," he said.

The next summer season saw another farce No Sex Please We're British, grace the theatre's stage.

Jessie Matthews was to have taken the lead role here but fell ill before the 1974 run started and so was replaced by Pip Hinton. The company included Deal based Carry On actor Charles Hawtrey as well as Carol Hawkins and Peter Denyer who were appearing in TVs Fenn Street Gang at the time.

159. The Astroglide became a firm favourite after its 1973 arrival – allegedly in lieu of a debt to Dreamland.

160. Below: Yvonne Stagg, right, daredevil performer of the Wall of Death brought the motorbike show to the park in 1974. She is pictured with local grandmother Elizabeth Mendez who asked to be taken for a spin around it.

161. Right: Elizabeth Mendez tries one of the bikes for size with Yvonne and co-rider Cliff Cody. Tragically, in late 1976, Yvonne committed suicide at her home in Southend, Essex, after her lover Thomas Biebuyck was convicted of manslaughter for killing her former boyfriend and business manager Steven Kokos, from Westgate near Margate, in 1975.

In 1973 the decision was also taken to refurbish the ballroom and rename it The Topspot. After a two month long £30,000 restyling it opened with a concert by Georgie Fame followed the night after by The Tremeloes.

Billed as the most 'in' place in Kent for young people, it was equipped with nearly 1,000 lights connected by three miles of cable. More than 400 decorative lamps fixed to fade and flash were set under seating with another 400 in the stage wings able to colour pulse to sound. A projector threw patterns on the walls and stage while a second, fitted with a zoom lens, cast pictures on to a 26 feet wide screen.

One of the most successful events at Topspot was a concert by Rock & Roll King Bill Haley and the Comets who were beginning a 20th anniversary British tour in February 1974.

Rock Around The Clock, See You Later Alligator, Shake, Rattle and Roll, and Rip It Up featured that memorable night. Aside from Bill, then 47, the line up included two original Comets, Reynold Cawley on bass and Rudolph Pompili on saxophone.

Many of the audience came suitably dressed, men in long coats and drainpipe trousers and women in pencil skirts and fitted jackets. The happy audience included middle aged people but there were also many in their twenties too.

Topspot would see many big name groups during its four year life including The Drifters, Slade, The Marmalade, Suzi Quattro and Alvin Stardust.

New brooms herald a new era

162. *The top of the Astroglide offered a good view of the park but youngsters sliding down probably ignored it!*

Another attraction which quickly became a favourite was the Astroglide. This was a six lane, undulating, 50 feet high slide. Its polished plastic surface ensured fast riding – some of that seemingly spent airborne! – before landing among a heap of sprawling bodies at the bottom.

The River Caves ride was given a much needed overhaul as it marked its 50th anniversary. During the work a teaspoon marked Wembley Exhibition 1924 was discovered in the structure.

A beer festival was held for the first time at Dreamland in 1972. This one day event proved such a success that it became a two day occasion in August 1973 when the Garden Café rang to the sound of hundreds of clinking glasses as mighty thirsts were quenched. Four breweries, Bass Charrington, Ind Coope, Truman and Whitbread, were invited to ply their wares during the two days bringing with them traditional horse drawn drays which were paraded through the town. By the end some 25 barrels – or 7,200 pints – had been consumed and such was the event's popularity that beer festivals continued at Dreamland until 1978.

The 1973 event was opened by comedian and radio presenter Charlie Chester. Afterwards Doug Harrison said: "Our confidence in extending the beer festival has been well justified. It is not only sales that matter – we have provided a further attraction for holiday makers right in the peak of the summer season."

The general state of the economy in the early 1970s made life difficult for most people and by now fewer staff were employed at the park. Before long nearly every Dreamland activity was being operated by a concessionaire – not only stalls and small rides but major rides and even the catering and cinema.

No longer able to retain 15 of the 35 ride attendants for maintenance work in the winter, a number of the long established rides were dismantled in the seventies and sold for little more than scrap value, among them the Racing Coaster, and the Miniature Railway, from which the sole steam engine Billie – Prince Edward of Wales having been disposed of in 1969 – was sold to the Marine Lake Railway, Rhyl, from where it originated.

163. *Eric Winter, who had operated the Racing Coaster for nine years prevously, looks on sadly as the ride is dismantled in 1975. Eric had worked for Dreamland since the 1930s.*

164 and 165. *Norman Wisdom brought slapstick comedy to the It's A Knockout contests in the coach park while appearing for the summer season in 1975 – despite the attentions of the 'constabulary'. Was Mr Grimsdale nearby?*

Since then Billie, a rare Barnes Atlantic loco, has returned to the east Kent village of Preston, near Wingham. Billie made a rare public appearance in June 2005 supporting the Save Dreamland Campaign at a steam engine rally in the village. In 2014 Billie had yet to find a new home and still resides at Preston, alongside dozens of traction engines and street organs.

Replacement rides were complex, ultra modern affairs such as the Orbiter, the Tip-Top and the Swirl whose maintenance was undertaken by their owners. These appealed to visitors but destroyed the even appearance of the park where the rides had always been surrounded by uniform wooden fences and lamp posts, set off by colourful flower beds and neatly trimmed hedges. At their peak, the gardeners were growing no less than 10,000 geraniums a year among many others, using three greenhouses located in the void space of the Scenic Railway.

Thursday night fireworks displays discontinued at the end of the 1973 season. The final straw was the cost of replacing the worn out seating edging the car park arena. This brought an end to a tradition which had marked the opening of Dreamland park and celebrated everything including 50 years of Scouting, Margate's Borough Centenary, Victories at War and all the royal births, weddings and coronations. These events had been preceded by, in the thirties, a marching display by a leading military band and, in the fifties, community singing with Margate Silver Band. It was temporarily replaced by a version of the It's A Knock Out television game and more than once in 1975 Norman Wisdom, then playing to full houses at the Lido, Cliftonville, could be counted upon to add to the excitement with his own brand of interference!

166. *The Paratrooper ride in full swing in 1973.*

167. *The Caterpillar was doing good trade in the 1970s.*

168. The Italian designed Cyclone cost £70,000 to install in 1975.

On the plus side £70,000 was spent on the Cyclone, an exciting gravity ride of Italian design which was sited near the Scenic Railway – close to the spot previously occupied by the Racing Coaster, which had been dismantled earlier in the year after more than 50 years use.

Animals were still in evidence at the Safari zoo in the early part of the decade but in 1974 gave way to a Monster Park and a Parrot Jungle, the former featuring half life size fibreglass reproductions of prehistoric creatures.

169. Large model dinosaurs roamed the park in 1974. This publicity photo shows one being offered a pint during that year's beer festival. The venture was not a success and real animals returned the following season.

170. Michael Frewer, who ran the Dreamland Zoo in 1975, views the long abandoned animal cages built at the back of the park by 'Lord' George Sanger. Now the only ones left of their kind, they were grade two listed in 2009.

Their lack of success prompted the return of a zoo for 1975 when control was given to Michael Frewer who brought his collection of wild and farmyard animals to the park. They were kept in same area where Sanger's menageries had once lived.

Among the wild animals in residence this year were a tiger called Prince and tigress Sheba, who was within weeks of giving birth to a cub. Two lions, a Chinese water deer, three pumas, two pelicans, a fox, a pony and a donkey could also be seen along with ducks, geese, goats rabbits and chickens. The area would be revamped again as Magicland in 1980 in an attempt to recreate the success of the Magic Garden. Many of the original set pieces had been stored but had either deteriorated or were considered too old fashioned to reuse. A new set of fairytale scenes, illuminated at night, was constructed but made little impact.

171. Catnapping in his cage is Prince the zoo's tiger.

172. A bear gets to grips with his enclosure.

New brooms herald a new era

173. Mayor of Margate Cllr John Jones, left, is joined by Dreamland managers in 1975, to ceremonially disconnect the DC current which was replaced by AC electricity. The site was connected to the substation in the High Street.

Any fears of Dreamland becoming a remote outpost of a large company were quashed at the beginning of 1975 when Associated Leisure formed a new division at Margate to coordinate its rapidly expanding activities. From its HQ, senior management oversaw operations at centres in Berwick-on-Tweed to the Isle of Wight and from Liverpool to Weymouth. This arrangement would last until 1980.

175. In the middle of this melée of youngsters is former Blue Peter host Valerie Singleton who joined them at Dreamland for a day out organised by the Licensed Victuallers' Association in 1975.

174. Some of the DC main switches and circuit breakers connecting to the park's best known rides.

Despite earlier plans to make Dreamland one of the world's best, there was now a creeping reluctance to continue investing in Margate, increasingly being seen as a declining holiday town. Cheap foreign holidays had markedly reduced the appeal and contributed to the vicious circle of fewer amenities, falling visitor numbers and anti-social behaviour by drunken teenagers.

176. Here's one we made earlier! Val Singleton poses with some of the group after a ride on the Scenic Railway.

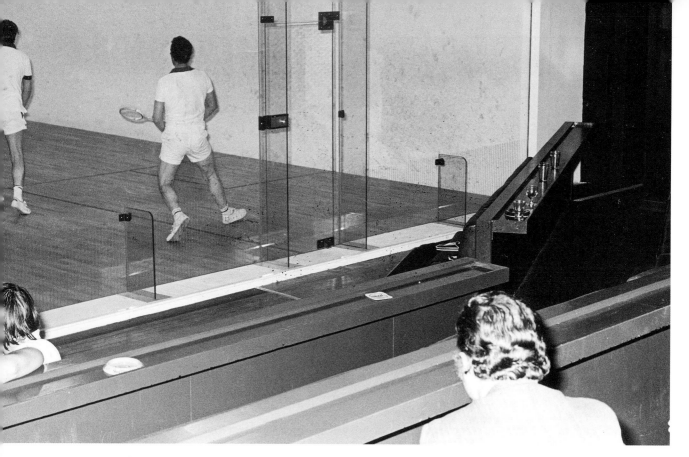

177. *A view into one of the glass fronted squash courts, taken soon after the opening in the late 1970s.*

178. *The Water Chute made a big splash from 1977.*

Associated Leisure decided to make its first ever investment in a sporting activity by spending £40,000 on the latest squash playing trend. In July 1977, four courts and a gymnasium were officially opened in the former Topspot by Kent and England cricketer Derek Underwood. This soon built up a club membership of 700. Two of the squash courts were glass fronted and a viewing gallery gave spectators the chance to see championship games.

Members were drawn from across East Kent competing in a number of local leagues. Increasing demand among players and beginners led to two more courts being added three years later as well as a small sports shop. These occupied the space taken by the gymnasium which transferred to the basement of the Tivoli Leisure Centre in Marine Terrace. The squash club would last for another 10 years, until November 1990, when falling membership made it no longer viable.

The latter part of the seventies saw the park being given something of a facelift, notably with the removal in 1977 of the Queen Mary centrepiece to help widen the entrance to the main attractions. In its place went 14 sideshows and a new dodgem car track.

Another new arrival this year was the Water Chute. There were only four in Britain at the time. The others were at Blackpool, Rhyl and

179. The Skywheels ride was dismantled and sold to a Dutch operator in 1977 after 24 years service in the park.

Portugal, where the ride was first introduced by inventor, Sir Leslie Joseph, in the mid thirties. A shareholder in Margate Estates in the 1950s, he supervised installation at Dreamland where it was operated as a joint venture with his company, Trust House Forte Leisure Ltd.

The ride had in fact been reconstituted from a partly burnt out one from Battersea Fun Fair. The six cars each carrying six passengers dropped from 50 feet into a 13,000 gallon tank of water, reaching a speed of around 45 miles per hour. The Cyclone ride was moved to another area of the park to make way for the Water Chute.

The facelift programme also saw the removal of the Skywheels which Jack Lynch had designed and built back in 1953. The Skywheels was bought by a Dutch operator and shipped to Holland along with Britain's only other example which came from Great Yarmouth, for a total of £12,000. This was a bargain price considering the Margate ride alone had cost £17,500 to construct.

The Garden Café hosted a summer season of weekly wrestling competitions for the first time in 1978 arranged by professional TV wrestler Jackie Pallo. The opening contest in July was a best selling success between him and lithe Jon Cortez but the limelight was taken by a ladies' contest between the well-built Miss Lena Blair and the slender Miss Cheeta. Eager crowds shouted their support and after a hectic tussle Miss Lena defeated her opponent by one fall and one submission to one fall.

1980 was the park's golden jubilee year and more attractions arrived now to help mark the anniversary. Numerous events and promotions offering discounted fares or free rides were held throughout the summer.

At the same time a fond farewell was bade to Doug Harrison in February when he retired after no less than 35 years working for Dreamland, the last nine as MD. He had certainly seen the best of years at the park and like John and Eric Iles before him had given his all to its continued success. Doug died in 1987, aged 68.

180. Lena Blair, left, and Miss Cheeta tussle during their bout in the Garden Café in 1978.

181. Managing Director of Dreamland, as well as the Lido, Cliftonville, was Doug Harrison. He joined the parent company, Margate Estates, in 1946 as a management trainee, working his way up through the ranks to become MD in 1971.

182. Advertising manager Mick Tomlinson made scale models of the park's rides. Here he displays his version of the Big Wheel with daughter Clare in 1980.

Among the publicity Dreamland's jubilee attracted was a celebratory supplement in the amusement trade newspaper World's Fair. On the back page of this editorial, a representative speaking for the Kent & Sussex section of the fairground concessionaires professional body said: "The park is still showing itself as the leader in this part of the country. There can be no doubt that Dreamland must play a major role in the general economy of the Thanet area.

"It attracts huge numbers of visitors, who of course, spend vast sums of money throughout the area – and not just at the amusement park alone."

These words were spoken by the man who would later take on the mantle of Dreamland ownership – one Jimmy Godden.

What was probably the biggest ride of them all turned up in golden jubilee year, the 180 feet high Big Wheel. This was added at a cost of £150,000, rotating up to 240 riders in its gondolas for a thrilling aerial view of Margate and was itself visible for miles around.

183. Tony Blackburn inspects the complete Dreamland model with Mick Tomlinson at a local trade exhibition in 1976.

New brooms herald a new era

184. A youthful Jim Davidson made a guest appearance to promote the Newice rink in 1980.

Unfortunately, the other main venture marking the park's jubilee would prove a distinct failure – the installation of a synthetic ice skating rink in the old Garden Café. Intended as a year round facility, 500 sq metres of polyethylene blocks of Newice were laid following encouragement by the local council. Key users were meant to be schools and youth clubs just as much as residents and visitors. One of only two in the country, it opened halfway through the 1980 season at a cost of £150,000 but survived for only 15 loss-making months by which time fewer than 200 people were using it at weekends.

Indeed, there was a feeling among some staff the Newice rink was never really meant to make a profit – merely just appear as a useful asset for any new owner in the event of a sale.

Whether or not it made any difference at all is unknown but in May 1981 Associated Leisure announced it had sold the freehold of Dreamland for £1.6 million to the Dutch amusement park operators, the Bembom family.

185. In 1980 sultry sisters Julie, left, and Dawn Stevens, variously Miss Broadstairs and Miss Margate, were also invited to try out the rink. Hopefully, it was a warm day.

186. The biggest of Big Wheels, at 180 feet high, made its Dreamland debut in 1980. Safety rails were later added to the gondolas to reduce the risk of a fall.

New brooms herald a new era

187. Willem, left, and Mathys Bembom took over running the park and are pictured in front of the new Ladybird ride in March 1982, just before opening for their first full season.

The Bembom years

The Bembom family already ran the Ponypark Holiday centre at Slagharen, in northern Holland, as well as two smaller parks – one near Marseilles and the other at Kirchhorst near Hanover.

The family's purchase of Dreamland was completed by November 1981 and two of the seven brothers, Willem and Mathys, sons of Henk, were put in charge working with general manager Alan Coppin who had succeeded Doug Harrison.

The Bembom Brothers were quick to realise that major changes to the park were necessary, both in terms of what it offered visitors and its own public image.

For a long time Dreamland had been tarnished by regular problems of drunken behaviour, vandalism and fighting. One of the first moves was to change the name to Bembom Brothers Theme Park. This didn't apply to the cinemas as they had been leased back to Associated Leisure

and so both names could be clearly seen on the side of the skyscraper building.

Bembom's other parks operated by charging an admission fee, allowing visitors free access to all the rides. It was proposed to introduce this to Margate and was a first in Britain. For the princely sum of £2.50, the whole park was yours for the day. There was some local scepticism about such a scheme but the Bemboms correctly assessed that a controlled admission system, with potential trouble makers barred, would encourage business.

Since alcohol contributed to the disorders of the past, the bars around the park were closed, and this applied to the seafront buildings which, again, were leased back to Associated Leisure. The Bemboms also abandoned evening opening – closing at 6pm – thus not only making considerable savings in power and wages, but also avoiding vandalism which had become a serious problem after dark. In any case, most

188. The cinema building bearing both Dreamland and Bembom Brothers signage on a gloomy day in the late 1980s.

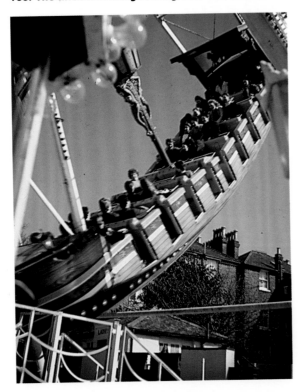

visitors to Margate were day trippers who started leaving for home at around this time anyway.

Operation of the rides and sideshows was taken back by the Bemboms with the concessionaires, naturally disgruntled, being told to remove their equipment. This would be gradually replaced by impressive thrill rides such as the Looping Star from Germany whose cars looped the loop, a replica of the Mary Rose which carried 40 passengers through a complete orbit and a swinging Pirate Ship, which merely travelled through 180 degrees!

The Wave Swinger, a gigantic Chair-o-Plane whose central stem moved, was installed for the 1984 season. This increased the number of rides to around 30 which now spread on to the coach park. The nearby former Margate station goods yard was bought for £125,000 to provide extra parking. Later, this was redeveloped for housing.

189. The Pirate Ship, Hanseatic, came complete with German signage upon its arrival in Margate. It was able to replicate sailing in a force 12 gale.

190. *The German made Looping Star combined with the Big Wheel to make a dramatic impact on the park's skyline when it arrived for the 1982 season.*

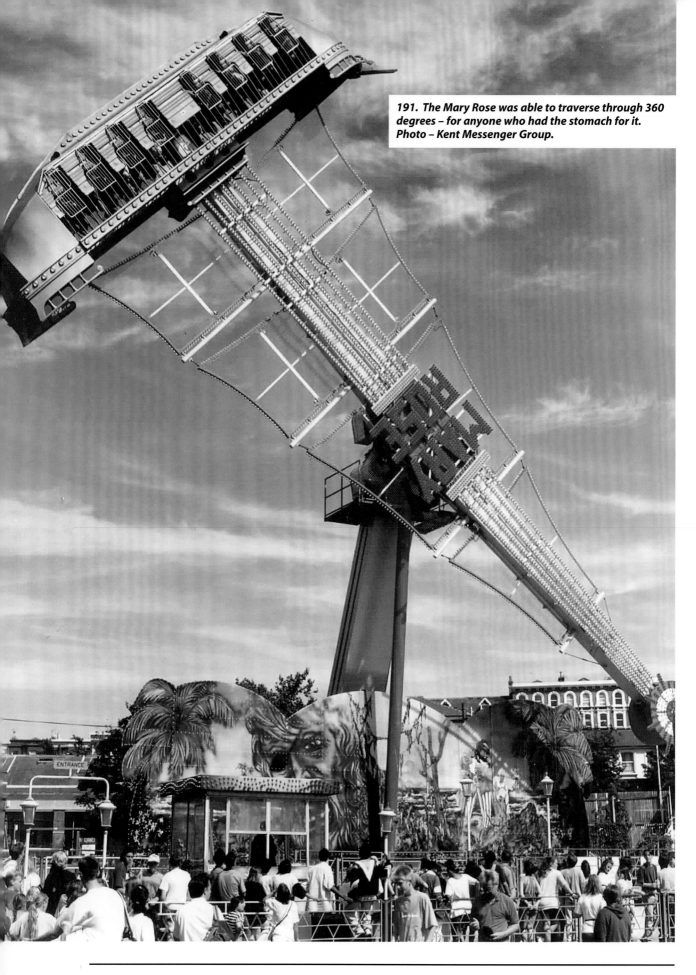

191. The Mary Rose was able to traverse through 360 degrees – for anyone who had the stomach for it. Photo – Kent Messenger Group.

192. The Cinema 2000 boasted the world's largest screen and showed 3-D action films to willing audiences.

Even small children benefited from modern rides, including a little motor cycle track with 10 mini Yamaha bikes. The whole park was also completely resurfaced.

Bringing this new lease of life to Dreamland was fully justified in the first few seasons with attendances of nearly two million a year. The one price concept spread to other British amusement parks whose operators could see improved cash control, security and far simpler administration.

Among the millions now visiting Dreamland were dozens of Muslims arriving from London, some in large chauffeur driven limousines.

To encourage them further, the brothers decided a grassy 80 sq yard area of the park should be set aside to enable them to pray facing Mecca.

General manager Alan Coppin told the Thanet Times in August 1984: "Some wear Western clothes and many are accompanied by their wives in full yashmaks. They enjoy the thrills and excitement because there is nothing like this in the Middle East.

"We are now considering how we can serve the Arabs better and are thinking of introducing a kebab restaurant as well as the private area where they can make their devotions to Mecca. It can be a bit embarrassing for them in the middle of the park.

"We are anxious to cater for their needs, but we don't want to upset people nor do we want it all to be a joke."

Nonetheless, a Thanet Council spokesman was quoted in the Daily Mail, who picked up on the story, saying Margate would now have to swop its beach donkeys for camels.

1985 saw the Golden Jubilee of the cinema's opening and was celebrated in style with the return of Lewis Gerard from his home in Santa

193. The Ladybird, a modern roller coaster for kids, was introduced to Bembom's in time for the 1983 season.

Barbara, California, to play the Compton organ one more time.

Lewis flew into a British winter from an 87 degree climate in the US and promptly caught a chill. Swift action with a visit to a local chemist saved the day and Lewis was able to play a two hour concert suitably decongested.

Fully restored variously by the Medway and Margate Theatre Organ Clubs, the Compton excited all who attended this special event. Lewis paid tribute to those who had looked after the organ saying it had played 1,000 times better than in 1935. Lewis visited Dreamland again in 1994 before dying the following year, aged 84.

New attractions came and went. Two of the most notable farewells were those of the River Caves and the neighbouring Sphinx in 1984. Rising maintenance costs and the pressing need for something new combined to see them off. Sadly, both attractions were simply demolished with no attempt made to salvage any of their more evocative components.

Continuing the trend to cater for younger children as well as adults, other arrivals in the 1980s included the Ladybird – a twisty, turning roller ride with cars painted like the black and red insect – and the Enterprise, with its

suspended cars swinging through 180 degrees. For those preferring to keep their feet firmly on the ground, the 3-D Cinema 2000 provided thrills in a large orange and white tent showing car chases spliced with sequences from white knuckle rides.

The Bembom brothers kept the park in good

194. Another youngsters' ride was the Big Apple.

The Bembom years

195. A bird's eye view of the Scenic Railway and the Heat Wave taken from the Big Wheel in the mid 1980s.

shape and succeeded in giving it a much needed new perception in the view of the paying public and it had rightly become one of the 10 most visited tourist attractions in the UK by the late 1980s.

The park achieved lasting fame at Christmas 1989 when BBC's festive episode of Only Fools and Horses, The Jolly Boys Outing, was screened on TV for the first time. Centred around a day trip to Margate which goes spectacularly wrong for Del Boy, Rodney and friends, several of the key rides including the Scenic Railway and the Mary Rose were featured – and looked in first class order.

But the Dreamland name wouldn't go away – somehow telling friends you were going to Bembom's never did sound particularly exciting – and so the old name was reintroduced in 1990 to local delight. By now it cost £5.99 each to enjoy the rides.

The Sunshine Room in the cinema building now became Coco's children's indoor play park, with lots of climbing equipment and multi-coloured ball ponds. It proved an ideal place for youngsters to enjoy an afternoon, especially if going for a birthday party. Below it, the former Bali Hai bar was turned into an arcade.

Greenery was once again recognised as an important ingredient in making the park a

196. The Sphinx was a fixture for many years, only disappearing in the late 1980s.

cheerful place. Frank Buttery, a long serving employee who had become operations manager, was able to tell the Isle of Thanet Gazette in 1993 that more vegetation would make a pleasant change to the drab concrete which proliferated. Early on that year he said they had already planted 25 additional trees and extra flower beds.

Return to Bemboms' of the cinema building's lease in 1992 prompted an extensive refurbishment programme. Nearly £400,000 was spent on transforming the 850 seat bingo hall into one of the most luxurious of its kind in the county. Keeping faith with the past, the scheme attempted to retain the original Art Deco atmosphere alongside new seats, carpets and computerised electronics.

Happily, two statues dating back to the building's Hall By The Sea days were uncovered, restored and placed on either side of the stage to gaze down upon the players.

The management also took the chance to add a small dance floor in front of the caller's podium to use during tea dances which were being reintroduced at the time with the idea that music would be provided by the Compton organ.

As Steven Spielberg's dinosaur epic Jurassic Park was released so a year long programme to refurbish the cinemas was completed in 1993. This £200,000 transformation took a long time to finish because the cinemas remained open throughout the work. It was the first time they had been upgraded on such a scale since

197. A 1989 close up view of the Looping Star. Judging by the queue, it was still pulling in big crowds. Photo – Kent Messenger Group.

twinning in the 1970s. Acres of new carpet were fitted along with a computerised ticket system and a cosy bar. A new Dolby stereo sound system was added as well.

To celebrate the occasion 14 films were shown non stop in one day for just 99 pence. One couple got their money's worth seeing them all running from 10am to close down at 11.30pm! Jurassic Park incidentally showed to packed houses during a four week spell in the summer.

In 1995, Dreamland was 75 years old and the all wooden Scenic Railway went into the Guinness Book of Records as the oldest roller coaster in the country. Some refurbishment work was carried out around the park's entrance tunnel at the beginning of what was planned to be another gradual redevelopment programme. This was also the year free admission returned to the park with the rides categorised according to age or height suitability.

More and more people were finding fixed entry price becoming expensive, admitted managing director Bob de Boer, especially if some members of the family or group didn't want to go on very many rides.

The return of free admission saw Bemboms' management buying neighbouring businesses, including the Cinque Ports pub on the opposite side of Hall By The Sea Road. This plan had cost £1 million itself and the park improvements would add another £500,000. Subsequently, the pub was sold to local pub chain Thorley Taverns who renamed it the Punch and Judy.

198. Riders hold on tight in this mid 1980s view of the Looping Star. Photo – Kent Messenger Group.

199. The scene in the park while building work was under way to replace miles of electrical cables and lay 100,000 block paving bricks in early 1996.

To the Millennium – and beyond

Three days before Christmas 1995 it was announced the Bembom family had sold Dreamland to established arcade and fairground owner Jimmy Godden. Already owner of the Rotunda amusement park in Folkestone, plus numerous arcades there as well as in Thanet and Dover, hopes were high for a bright future.

Bought for an undisclosed sum, further development of the park was assisted by a £450,000 grant from the Single Regeneration Budget – European money awarded to areas in need of improvement – while Thanet Council chipped in with another £50,000. Another £800,000 was added via a Regional Selective Assistance Grant.

This public money represented nearly 10 per cent of the total £5 million investment made by Jimmy Godden over the winter break as the park was given a new look and new rides were installed.

From now on, the site was to be known as The New Dreamland Fun Park, suggesting a shift away from the white knuckle emphasis placed on it by the Bemboms, to a more family oriented pleasure park.

Builders were hard at work with a major project as the New Year began, which became larger and cost more than originally planned, to tear up the park's Tarmac hardstanding, replace 12 miles of below surface electrical cabling and lay 100,000 block paving bricks. To the chagrin of some, the resurfacing also saw the disappearance of any remaining garden space.

Reopening was scheduled for the Easter weekend at the end of March 1996. Attractions ready to make their debut at Dreamland included a twin drop Log Flume water ride, a Bounty ship swing boat – similar to Bembom's Hanseatic of a decade before – two dodgem tracks, the return of a Waltzer and an Italian made Space Station, which was the first in Britain.

Five more children's rides were added while an American style 12 hole illuminated mini golf course would take its place in May. For those not wanting to ride, a 12,000 sq ft undercover arcade and shopping mall was created from the buildings by the main entrance in Hall By The Sea Road.

Publicity announcing the dream was coming alive once more said the Scenic Railway had also

200. Sir Bob Geldof, with daughter Fifi Trixibelle, 13, her friend Lewis Cady and Bob's then girlfriend actress Jeanne Marine, get a soaking on the newly installed Log Flume in 1996. Sir Bob was later given the park's first, and only, lifetime free pass.

been refurbished and that 140 gallons of red and cream paint had been used smartening up the 180 feet high Big Wheel.

Colin Dawson had joined as Dreamland Leisure's new managing director after being headhunted from Thorpe Park. He pointed out at the time: "On one hand we are bringing the park up to date with a range of new ideas. On the other we are turning back the clock to that glorious heyday when a million people a year enjoyed the unique Dreamland experience."

Admission to the park continued to be free while access to rides was by purchasing plastic tokens at 70p each or Ride All Day Wristbands at £10 for adults or £7 for children.

Heavy snowfalls in the winter months put back building work by more than a week and despite the contractors working around the clock, the park wasn't as ship shape as the management had hoped for by the Easter opening. Rather than cancel, the price of wristbands was halved for the weekend.

Colin Dawson said in a press release: "We moved heaven and earth to get the park ready in time. The majority of our visitors were delighted by the transformation. The new Log Drop was an instant hit and has been in constant demand. It was also good to see queues for the Scenic Railway and the Big Wheel."

Bright sunshine over the Easter weekend ensured bumper crowds and by the end of the four day break, around 30,000 people had enjoyed Dreamland's delights, a good result.

For the first time in years, probably since before the Bembom ownership, the park stayed open in the evenings. Friday Fun Nights, with cut price ride tokens for Thanet residents, quickly proved a success and ran throughout May and June. It was billed as a form of thank you to regular customers supporting Dreamland since it reopened after the facelift.

Engineers working on the installation of a new £500,000 dark ride called the Stowaway – a modern version of the much missed River Caves – downed tools after they claimed to have been spooked by a ghost.

They had been working in the arcade area close to the seafront entrance and as they dug down to install the Stowaway's water feature had opened up an access tunnel originally used during the Sanger days. This was the spot where a young woman had been murdered by the Margate strongman in 1895 (see page eight).

Dreamland engineer Trevor Naylor and Dan Tippetts from theme park consultants Farmer Studios said the strange noises and sensations they had experienced were too much for them and they would not be going back on the night

To the Millennium – and beyond

shift until something was done. They had both suddenly felt cold there as if they had walked straight into a fridge. Ghostly props forming part of the ride only made matters worse for them!

An urgent appeal went out to find anybody who could calm the situation and allow work on the new ride to continue. In May, clairvoyant Mia Dolan visited the park to help exorcise the ghost, which she said at the time, was indeed that of the fated young woman.

Mia explained afterwards: "Local legend says she was a prostitute but she wasn't. She was a showman's daughter who was raped by the strongman then left for dead in one of the tunnels. It appears she returned to put the record straight and clear her name."

The girl's appearance had previously been documented in The Guardian in August 1990 when amateur ghost hunter Andrew Green was called to the park after other sightings. He said at the time: "This is genuine. There is something happening." The Stowaway, meanwhile, was ready for use only a week late.

In June 1996, the Scenic Railway carried a distinguished visitor, the then Heritage Secretary Virginia Bottomley, who officially reopened the park. Only a few weeks later the Scenic was the centre of attention again when 100 members of the American Coaster Enthusiasts Club visited to enjoy a ride.

Texan organiser Tim Baldwin explained the 76 year old ride's particular appeal: "There are some naughty little places where riders actually pop off their seat. We call that air-time and we just can't get enough of it. There isn't any air-time on American rides any more. There are so many safety harnesses holding you in, that you don't move an inch."

A £200,000 Skymaster ride returned to Dreamland during the season after spending the previous 18 months touring Thailand. It proved to be the park's biggest attraction for many – while leaving others completely dumbfounded at how anybody could stand being turned upside down as it rotated through 360 degrees to a height of 70 feet.

If anybody was doubting how successful the revived park would be, then those fears were laid to rest when it was announced that record arrivals during the last week of July saw wristbands almost run out. Emergency supplies were collected while another batch of 200,000 arrived shortly after.

Warm weather not only saw thousands coming through the gates but had an unusual effect on one of the rides. The exceptional heat on an August Sunday saw operators turning fire hoses on the Big Wheel as its metal structure started to expand and put it in danger of buckling slightly and becoming out of true. This would be the first of several such incidents.

The first season under Jimmy Godden's ownership was, by any standards, a successful one and the park continued to be a promising venture.

Maintenance during the close season revealed that of the park's 48,000 light bulbs, around 9,000 had to be replaced – not exactly light work, quipped Roy Vinson, who led a team of electricians who had been shinning up ladders and dangling from scaffolding to do the work.

Dreamland would take a starring role on TV in 1997 when it was used as the backdrop for the unexpectedly successful Channel Four drama, Underworld. The cast included Annette Crosbie, James Fleet and Susan Wooldridge who visit Margate to relive their childhood but are instead sucked into a lawless alien world. Large crowds

201. Stomach churning rides like the Skymaster helped draw considerable numbers after its arrival in 1996.

202. *The park was all lit up while filming night time scenes for Channel Four's Underworld in 1997.*

became unpaid extras during night time filming sessions. People queued four deep around the park until midnight for free rides on the Sky Master, Scenic Railway and others. Management reported more people had gone through the gates in two hours than on the busiest bank holidays.

In November 1997, the Big Wheel, by now as much a landmark of Dreamland as the cinema building, was taken down and sold to the Groupo Magico theme park in Mexico City. It was a long job. Dismantling the wheel, its gondolas and the massive supports took more than a month for three large cranes. Eventually, it was carried off in 18 lorry loads to the Isle of Grain for shipment to Mexico.

Colin Dawson said at the time: "It was a difficult decision to make but times change and visitors are demanding bigger and better thrills. "We're sorry to see the wheel go but it was no longer attracting sufficient numbers to justify the amount of space it takes up in the park."

The wheel had in fact been up for sale for a year previously and enquiries had come from all over the world, including South Africa, Singapore, Spain and Australia. A deal to sell to America fell through when the prospective new owner failed to get planning permission to rebuild it in the US.

203. *Even as it was being dismantled, the Big Wheel still managed to look imposing.*

To the Millennium – and beyond

204. *The Wild Mouse was introduced to Margate in 1998 and caused a sensation among eager visitors.*

The Big Wheel made way for a new £1 million Wild Mouse ride which arrived in May 1998 from its German manufacturers. This 'rodent coaster' had eight cars, each seating four people and was able to carry 1,000 people every hour. The bright yellow structure measured 40 metres by 18 metres and stood 15 metres high.

Heightened security surrounded its arrival. Dreamland staff were sworn to secrecy about the plans and the components arrived in nine large lorries under cover of darkness and took 10 days to build.

Elsewhere, the former Sunshine Café was proving popular as the venue for the relaunched adventure park for younger children. Picking up on the popularity of Mr Coco's during the earlier part of the decade, it was now known as the Adventure Zone. Fully trained staff and cushioned floors ensured nobody came a cropper while clambering across a rope walkway, slipping down slides or bounding into a ball pit. The neighbouring Wizard of Dreams diner revived the youngsters – and no doubt proved an ideal bolt hole for the grown ups!

A gang of Elvis impersonators took over the park in July for a bizarre bachelor party. Twenty Elvises enjoyed some of the first rides on the newly installed Cosmic Cannon – a reverse bungee jump style ride which involved people being catapulted 160 feet high in 1.5 seconds inside a tiny capsule.

Not something for the faint hearted – as Dreamland publicist John Nurden discovered. His contract with the park's owners insisted he try out all new rides and the management held him to this condition when the cannon arrived.

A white faced John said after his ordeal: "The management spend the winter hatching up new ideas for rides and then watch with glee as I'm strapped in!"

It wasn't the first time he had to endure this occupational hazard – two years before he, with Colin Dawson, had to pose for photographers at the top of the Big Wheel after both admitted they were frightened of heights.

Illuminations from Blackpool brought some added sparkle to Dreamland when it reopened for 1999. Light bulb characters of clowns and policemen were among the 12 custom made displays purchased from the north west resort and proved a success during Friday evening openings.

Eight more rides, costing a total of £2 million, were added as well including a Mirror Maze, a King Kong themed ghost train and the return of a Looping Star ride, first made popular by Bemboms in the 1980s. The Loop's comeback now gave Dreamland no less than five rollercoaster rides for visitors to choose from.

205. A view of the park in summer 1999 just after the arrival of a new, but smaller than previous, Looping Star seen furthest away in this photo. On the left is the still popular Ladybird ride.

Over the years, Dreamland had built up a sound tradition for hosting large groups of children who either had disabilities or were from under privileged backgrounds. In previous times the Licensed Victuallers' Association or the Albany Taxi charity had brought youngsters from London and beyond for a day out in Margate. This tradition continued in May 1999 with a third annual convoy of 100 Saab convertibles, organised by the Lady Taverners, departing from an East London dealership to bring 200 children to Dreamland. The event continued to be a popular one for at least two more seasons by which time up to 500 youngsters were being driven to Margate.

206. The four actors who featured as the Dream family in the park's first ever TV advert.

The drive to bring more visitors to Dreamland shifted up a gear with the making of a 20 second TV advert in July sharing a £100,000 budget with Folkestone's Rotunda.

Four actors were recruited to portray the ideal family with Stephen Picton as dad, Hilary Watkins as mum, eight year old Natalie Gower and her real life 10 year old brother Oliver, both from Westgate, as the children.

While the youngsters relished the chance of several free goes on the Scenic Railway, the Wild Mouse and the Looping Star during filming, it proved a tougher challenge for Stephen who revealed the director insisted they rode the Loop six times and the Mouse four times before getting the perfect take.

"I was bounced all over the place and bruised every bone in my body. People who ride these things for enjoyment must be out of their minds! It was the first time I'd been to a fun park in 15 years. I'd forgotten what these rides can be like," he said afterwards.

By now Dreamland was the county's second most visited tourist attraction after Leeds Castle, near Maidstone, so there was some frustration by the management when it was realised it had been left out of a glossy tourism brochure designed to entice visitors to Kent.

Colin Dawson departed the company in February 2000, a completely amicable arrangement said a press announcement at the time, to concentrate on a new internet service in London. He would remain a consultant for the rest of the year.

207. TV twins Melanie and Martina Grant helped celebrate the Year of the Carousel on one of Dreamland's restored roundabouts. The park had four different versions, one of which was 100 years old at the time.

In the same month it was announced that Dreamland Leisure had bought the former PAB Electronics factory bordering the park by the Belgrave Road entrance in hope of turning it into a food outlet, to redress the decline of quality gift shops and cafes in the vicinity. Permission for change of use was granted in April.

In the fairground world, the Millennium year was declared the Year of the Carousel. As they were a personal favourite of Jimmy Godden, Dreamland took a full part promoting all four of its rides, which included a newly arrived traditional style three-abreast version and an existing 100 year old four-abreast roundabout whose 76 horses had been given a full makeover.

In January 2001 the Isle of Thanet Gazette announced Jimmy Godden's company was talking with a leading supermarket, thought to be Morrisons, to sell some of the park's land including the old electronics factory, for a new store. While true, the talks eventually came to nothing.

Seven more rides provided a much needed boost in time for the new season's start including a larger version of the Looping Star, the previous one having already been dismantled, and a 49 feet high Frisbee ride to replace the Sky Master. A 17 metre high Sling Shot was able to take 12 people at a time to the top of its tower and drop them back to earth in moments. The Cosmic Cannon made way for an even more powerful 125 feet high Ejection Seat, costing £150,000. A new Pirate Ship ride took the place of the Bounty swing ship.

With Millenium celebrations now well and truly over, Jimmy Godden announced the company had purchased, at a knockdown auction price, 600,000 surplus Millennium Dome souvenirs. Among this haul were 200,000 badges, 100,000 key rings, the same of rubbers, 307 rubbish bins and 2,500 pairs of black trousers! Four lorries brought the goodies to Margate, mostly for use as prizes in the arcade machines.

208. Jimmy Godden with just a handful of the 600,000 surplus Millennium Dome souvenirs he bought.

209. Waltzer rides had been a familiar sight at Dreamland for decades. An electrical fault set fire to this one on a Sunday afternoon in November 2003.

210. Clear track ahead – a front seat view on the Scenic Railway, which became a listed structure in 2002.

By now it was plain to see for even the most casual observer that things were very different from their 1950s heyday. Large open spaces were appearing where there had previously been rides and the overall impression was one of a lack of tender loving care, despite substantial investment.

Considering this, visitor numbers were holding up well at 700,000 for both 2001 and 2002 seasons.

Despite widespread positive publicity when the Scenic Railway was given Grade II listing in March 2002 – the first amusement park ride in the country to be accorded this status – Jimmy Godden's company announced at the beginning of 2003 the park might close forever at the end of that summer season and be redeveloped into shops and leisure units by the Stadium Group.

A strong Save Dreamland Campaign mobilised and quickly gained 13,000 supporters from far and near. The campaign won a great deal of media coverage, lobbying decision makers and holding regular meetings with leaders at Thanet Council.

Campaign mastermind Nick Laister, an Oxfordshire based planning consultant and amusement park preservationist, found a French operator willing to take over the park that year but ultimately this move did not progress.

Showman David Wallis leased the park from Jimmy Godden for the 2003 season and proved Dreamland was still a viable proposition – and more so if only some investment could be made.

The Scenic Railway was operated as a separate concession, after appropriate safety work had been carried out, and was in use by May. Initially, there was talk of forming a separate preservation trust for the ride but this plan fell apart during the summer when it was realised £5,000 in takings could not be accounted for.

In spring 2004 Philip Miller, the operator of Southend's Adventure Island theme park, made an offer of 'at least' £10 million for Dreamland, promising to spend that much again on new rides – but he was turned away with Jimmy Godden stating the park was worth at least five times that figure.

There were real fears the park wouldn't open at all for the 2004 season but Dreamland did eventually welcome visitors for July and August with David Wallis once again leasing the site. It was too late though for the many people who arrived in Margate over the Easter holiday in search of fun, to find the park gates firmly shut. Local businesses and media expressed concern – not for the first time – that Dreamland's closure would sound the death knell for the town's viability as a tourist venue.

By now the Save Dreamland Campaign was fully involved in giving evidence to a public enquiry hearing objections to the Thanet Local Plan and the Margate Masterplan – a proposed regeneration scheme for the future of the town centre and seafront. In this, Thanet Council, after saying for a long time it wanted to see the entire park site stay in leisure use, had a change of heart.

The council was roundly criticised by the campaign for this move and even English Heritage joined in suggesting, in a letter to the enquiry, that the public had been misled over the future of the Scenic Railway. Under cross examination, the council admitted it had no evidence saying Dreamland was not viable.

The council reported back on the public's responses to the Masterplan and revealed that 44 per cent of the replies concerned Dreamland. Almost all supported use of the site as a major amusement park.

The report stated: "The public sees the Dreamland site as Margate's key potential tourism/leisure generator, and closure of the facility is seen as highly negative for the town's future."

Early 2005 saw the Wild Mouse and Regatta rides being removed and sold to Loudon Castle theme park in Scotland – owned by Henk Bembom.

In March, news broke that Jimmy Godden had sold Dreamland for an undisclosed sum. The new owner was the Margate Town Centre Regeneration Company. It was a combination of Margate Development Limited, which had a 60 per cent share, and Jimmy Godden who retained a 40 per cent interest. Margate Development was owned by Toby Hunter, the major shareholder in Newbury based firm Waterbridge, and businessman David Schriber.

Jimmy Godden said at the time: "I have basically sold out at Dreamland. New people are coming in to regenerate the park and move it forward. I will be taking very much a back seat."

Toby Hunter declined to reveal how much was paid for the site saying only "several, several, several millions." Later this was suggested by local media as being £20 million.

211. A 2002 view inside the new Oriental Buffet restaurant. Compare this scene to the opening of the Sunshine Café in 1934. Photo – Kent Messenger Group.

212. Detail of carousel horses on the three abreast roundabout just before the season's close in 2003. Photo – Nick Evans/Kent Messenger Group.

213. A maintenance team gets stuck into carrying out repairs to the Scenic Railway ahead of the 2005 season. Photo – Kent Messenger Group.

214. An art project in spring 2006 saw billboard sized pictures affixed to the cinema building as its distinctive signage had been taken down for repair. A big wheel temporarily occupied a space between two neighbouring arcades creating this striking view along the seafront.

He said what would eventually replace the park was not yet decided as his company wanted further discussions with Thanet Council.

He added the Scenic Railway could remain part of the development and his company would work with English Heritage and the council to determine its future. He went on to say Dreamland was a key site and had an interesting part to play in the town's cultural and social development.

Meanwhile, showman Harry Ayers, who was running other attractions around the country, took over the park lease for the 2005 season and introduced several new rides including the Top Buzz, Drop Tower and Log Coaster. With £20,000 also spent on ensuring the Scenic Railway was safe once more, all seemed set for a good season running from late May to early September.

That promise soon evaporated when admission charges were introduced for the first time in many years. Realising they were a deterrent, the charges were dropped part way through the season. For those who did venture in, the selection of rides made it a pleasurable half day trip but it was abundantly clear the glory days were not going to return.

Poor marketing, and rejections of offers to be highlighted on TV news programmes, meant many people living outside Thanet had little or no idea the park was open for business.

After a long wait of more than a year the government inspector's interim report into the Thanet Local Plan Enquiry – to which the Margate Masterplan was linked – was published in September 2005. His interim report said retail development of the park site would not be appropriate and he recommended the council's stance on allowing houses and shops to be built there should be modified accordingly.

His recommendations were not binding on Thanet Council and it seemed likely his advice would be ignored – which would have been a near unprecedented move.

In early 2006 a full council meeting agreed, after a heated debate between the two main political parties, that part of the site should be retained for leisure use and the rest redeveloped for shops or housing. An ensuing public consultation showed that the vast majority of residents felt the park was too important to be lost for yet more houses and 350 formal objections were handed over by the Save Dreamland Campaign in March 2006.

The park managed to open for a short season and a big wheel made a return for the first time in nine years. This wheel was placed in a space known locally as Godden's Gap, which had been created between two seafront buildings on Marine Terrace after one of the businessman's arcades burnt down in a spectacular fire in April 2003. Initially a success, it transpired the wheel had been double booked to a park in Scotland for two weeks in June. It was duly taken down, never to return.

Showman George Webb had rented the park but bad weather put plans back for a week. At the end of the season he reported: "The season has been good. There have been some days where the weather has been against us, but on one Saturday there were 14 coaches from London and that was in the pouring rain."

When the season finished in September the park became a film set for a couple of weeks as Channel Four filmed a production entitled Margate Exodus. The centrepiece was an 80 feet high Waste Man, designed by Anthony Gormley, sculptor of the Angel of the North, with the story being a modern retelling of how Moses led the Israelites out of Egypt and slavery. The filming culminated by burning the figure in front of a crowd of thousands, many of them recruited as extras in the production itself. Perhaps prophetically, fire crews were on hand to liberally douse the wooden Scenic Railway, just 50 yards away, amid real fears it would catch light too.

Margate Town Centre Regeneration Company now launched its own consultation to ask people what they would like to see happen on the site.

Lasting eight weeks, nearly 200,000 people were invited to put forward their opinions by phone, internet or face to face. The survey's key questions were criticised by the Save Dreamland Campaign as they failed to name the site in the text and quickly described the project as 'worthless'.

More than 700 people replied – a remarkably low number considering the amount of media coverage it was given – and provisional plans based on those responses were unveiled in March 2007 at public meetings in Margate's Winter Gardens by MTCRC's Toby Hunter. A new city by the sea was the main theme of the model presented to the event's visitors which kept a strong leisure aspect but allowed for some housing redevelopment. Finalised versions of the scheme, drawn up by London based DLA Architecture went on public view at Dreamland the following month.

215. Standing at 80 feet tall, the Waste Man designed by Anthony Gormley was the same height as the cinema building's iconic fin.

During April, SDC unveiled its own Vision for Dreamland which revealed for the first time a scheme to turn the site into the world's first heritage theme park.

Nick Laister said at the time: "The site would include some of the remaining examples of Britain's amusement park heritage, in a high quality park-like environment around the Scenic Railway.

"The listed cinema building would also be brought back into use with rides, shows, bars, restaurants and an amusement park or seaside heritage museum.

"Our position right at the start of this campaign was that some of the park could be redeveloped if it ensured the long term survival of the park.

"We see funding from the developer, along with other grant funding, as critical in delivering this attraction. The park could then be owned and potentially operated by a trust, after which it would be self-sufficient."

The concept quickly gained favour with local authorities and talks were soon under way with fairgrounds facing closure about bringing some of their older rides to Margate.

As far as site operations were concerned, 2007 was notable for three things, closure of the bingo club in May after 40 years, the park not opening for the summer at all and, in November, closure of the cinema complex.

Leaseholders Reeltime decided that competition from a newly opened multi-screen cinema at Westwood Cross, near Broadstairs, was too great and put up the shutters after a special charity screening on November 1 of the 1957 comedy film The Smallest Show On Earth. Ironically, it tells the story of a cinema struggling to make ends meet. Filmgoers were greeted with champagne at the entrance and there was a standing ovation at the end for 81 year old Derek Ray, projectionist for the previous 28 years.

Speaking for his team, cinema manager Ray Jackson told the audience: "We are at a loss and are in mourning. To know that you will never walk back in and see the box office and a cosy foyer brings tears to our eyes."

It should also be noted that the Compton organ is still in situ in the bingo hall beneath and has not been played since October 2004. Now, there are real fears that lack of air movement in the building since the cinema's closure could allow mildew to harm the instrument's delicate workings.

216. A final goodbye from the team who worked at Dreamland cinema. Photo – Kent Messenger Group.

With the site now looking distinctly forlorn and unloved, the Dreamland saga hit a new low in early spring 2008. At around 4.30pm on Monday April 8 smoke and flames were spotted coming from the train shed on the Scenic Railway.

It quickly became obvious this was no small fire. Within 20 minutes around one third of the wooden structure was well alight and the pall of smoke could be seen from several miles away. Around 15 fire engines raced to the scene but some appeared to be hindered by low mains water pressure in the area before they could fully tackle the flames. A similar problem had arisen during previous Scenic blazes. As fire fighters fought for control, a large crowd gathered by the Eaton Road and Belgrave Road entrances while others secured a vantage point on the roof of Arlington House's multi-storey car park. The news quickly spread far and wide – even the following day's Edinburgh Evening News found a small space to include a brief mention of the drama.

Margate was deeply shocked – many felt an old friend had been lost – and there was plenty of speculation about how it might have started. It was confirmed shortly after it was started deliberately. Not only had the fire ripped though key parts of the structure but all of the ride's original trains had been completely destroyed.

217. In October 2004 organist Nigel Ogden, right, would be the last professional to play the cinema's Compton organ. Photo – Kent Messenger Group.

218. The flames begin to take hold around the Scenic Railway's station platform area. By the time the fire had been extinguished some hours later, much of the signage seen here and the woodwork behind it had been destroyed. Photo – Nick Evans/Kent Messenger Group.

219. The blackest of days for Dreamland and Margate as the Scenic Railway burned in April 2008. Some firemen were still arriving at the park when this dramatic scene was captured. Photo – Nick Evans/Kent Messenger Group.

220. Set back on a 12 feet high bank, the original, and now listed, Sanger cages were exposed for the first time in many years during 2008 after trees and ivy were cleared.

It was, without question, a setback for all concerned while Thanet Council, to its credit, voted to compulsorily purchase the entire site should the required repair work not be carried out by MTCRC.

Dreamland cinema's architectural importance was confirmed in late April 2008 when the Department for Culture Media and Sport announced that its grade II listing had been upgraded to a rarer II* rating. The extra star is awarded to only eight per cent of all listed buildings for particular architectural influences, in this case its early Expressionist and Art Deco features.

221. A model of the Scenic Railway was centrepiece of the Dreamcoaster exhibition at the Substation project space.

During the early summer, with feelings still running high over the fire, the Save Dreamland Campaign mounted its Dreamcoaster exhibition in Margate High Street's Substation project space of memorabilia and a room sized replica of the Scenic to ensure people would not forget the place and what it represents to the town. By the end of the week, more than 500 people had visited.

In September work was carried out to record and carefully remove the damaged parts of the Scenic after the council insisted that a 420 metre long metal fence should encircle it to prevent further attacks and vandalism. One local paper observed the £40,000 cost of the fence was the same price paid for the whole site by John Henry Iles in 1919.

It was while the fence was going up that workmen uncovered the original cramped Sanger era animal cages at the rear of the park, closest to the railway line. Covered by ivy and trees, they had lain forgotten for at least 20 years and, according to the Bartlett Society which records the early history of zoos, were the only ones of their kind left in the world. A six month temporary listing was quickly served by Thanet Council.

Full listing was granted in February 2009 by the Department for Culture, Media and Sport stating: "Pleasure ground related structures are very rare, and early animal cages are exceptionally so."

A detailed business plan for the heritage theme park, which had been rapidly taking shape over the turn of the year, was unveiled in London during February 2009 by the newly created Dreamland Trust, a formal body born out of the

Save Dreamland Campaign. It appeared alongside plans drawn by theme park designer Jean-Marc Toussaint for how the site might eventually look. He had previously produced inspiring plans for the campaign in 2005.

The proposals were publicly revealed to a well attended 'I Dream of Dreamland' event in Margate during March. More than 400 supporters filled the West Coast Bar to see the drawings and enjoy a fun evening eating popcorn and candyfloss.

By May, a formal bid had been submitted to Sea Change for £4 million funding by the Dreamland Client Group, formed of the Dreamland Trust, MTCRC, Thanet Council and Margate Renewal Partnership.

Two months later, there was good news as the Heritage Lottery Fund announced it was granting £384,000 to help progress plans for the park's revival. In October HLF topped this up to £495,000. This first round success – effectively a major vote of confidence in the heritage park scheme – enabled it to move forward to the second stage of the HLF application process.

In November 2009, the Trust was able to announce its bid for £3.7m from the Sea Change fund had been successful – it was the largest grant awarded by the body whose role it was to help regenerate England's rundown seaside resorts. Hard on the heels of that announcement was that the Heritage Lottery Fund would support the Dreamland Trust with another £8m – once it had taken possession of the site.

Completing the first phase of reviving Dreamland was expected to cost around £12.4 million with the work centred around rebuilding the Scenic Railway and installing the historic rides already stored in Margate. It would also involve the restoration of the cinema building as a multi-purpose entertainment venue, creating a national centre for seaside heritage, popular culture and street style.

The Trust's Chairman Nick Laister summed up neatly at the time: "This proposal has the ability to create an outstanding 21st century attraction at Margate, capitalising on the resort's unique heritage in a way that will make a huge contribution to regeneration of the town."

222. An artist's impression by Jean-Marc Toussaint of how a rejuvenated River Caves ride might look in the plans for a Dreamland heritage theme park.

223. **The Scenic Railway as seen in September 2010 from the Arlington House flats side. Its listed status was uprated to the rarer Grade II* in July 2011 to put it on a par with the cinema building.**

Building a new dream

For the first time in several years, Dreamland appeared to have a real chance of being revived, with Easter 2011 quickly being talked about as a possible reopening date.

Alas, gaining possession of the Dreamland site would prove to be a long, arduous and unnecessarily protracted process. The plan was for Thanet Council, as fundholders, to purchase half of the site from Margate Town Centre Regeneration Company and then sell it on for a nominal sum to the Trust. MTCRC would retain the other half of the site for redeveloping into houses and shops.

Negotiations began in 2010 and initially progress was positive but broke down after a few months without agreement being reached. MTCRC was holding out for a high price reflecting the value of the site as housing and retail space rather than as a pleasure park. Meanwhile, work was carried out at the council's expense, under a series of urgent works notices, to the fabric of the cinema building repointing its millions of bricks and ensuring the roof kept the rain out.

With the 2011 opening date having slipped away, Thanet Council lost patience and on 3 June that year issued a compulsory purchase order for the entire Dreamland site.

Thus began a lengthy legal process of formal objection beginning with a public enquiry in January and February 2012 which saw Government approval that August, swiftly followed by another challenge from MTCRC and a subsequent High Court hearing in March 2013 lasting two days.

The High Court dismissed the challenge but, undeterred, MTCRC appealed against that during another High Court hearing in late May 2013 and was rebuffed once more.

224. **The blue wooden building seen in the photo above contains the driving gear to enable the Scenic's trains to climb the first hill.**

225. *Inside the bingo hall in September 2010 looking towards the stage. Most things had been left as they were since last used more than three years earlier – and that included the unemptied ash trays set into the tables.*

While the legal argument was going to and fro the Dreamland Trust felt confident enough of its case to announce, in October 2012, it was hiring Wayne Hemingway, fashion designer, co-founder of Red or Dead Design and mastermind of many successful vintage themed festivals, to create a vision for the new Dreamland.

A packed audience of nearly 150 gathered at the Turner Contemporary Gallery, at the other end of Margate's seafront, to see him unveil his ideas in

226. *This view of the bingo hall looks towards the entrances. It was created in 1973 from the stalls of the original cinema which saw the circle divided into twin cinemas – the ridged area of the hall's ceiling was the floor of the circle.*

227. The rear of the old ballroom, which forms part of the cinema building, is the oldest on the Dreamland site having been built in the 1860s as a railway station by the London Chatham and Dover Railway.

April 2013. He was quick to point out that he was not going to be simply recreating the Dreamland of the past but promised something new instead.

He stated: "We're not interested in bringing something back to life as it was because it very rarely works. The reason why something dies off is because society moves on.

"We'd like to take the best of the past, put it into a modern context and not lose sight of the DNA that made it great in the first place.

"This project is about place-making. We wouldn't be working on this project if Margate wasn't a place that had an opportunity to be something more special than it is now. It is on the march."

228. Wayne Hemingway outlines his plans for the new Dreamland during a packed event in April 2013.

In a subsequent magazine interview Wayne outlined his thoughts a little more saying: "There will be an element of revival, but great heritage must have a lasting appeal to future generations.

229. Despite appearances, this moulding is cleverly set into the cinema wall, not raised from it. Recorded in 2010 it was still in good condition having been covered up for nearly 40 years since creating the twin cinemas.

"We are aiming at an aspirational modern audience and we have to widen the appeal of Dreamland.

"It must also go beyond a seasonal attraction and I think it can mean something internationally. There will be rides of course, but it won't just be for kids. Look back at the old photos of Dreamland in the 1930s, you'll see that adults can have fun at the seaside too."

At this stage hopes were high for the park to be operational for the 2014 season but in June 2013, the Isle of Thanet Gazette revealed there had been a delay by the council in publishing its intention to serve a General Vesting Declaration on MTCRC – the document announcing its intention to take over the site. This oversight pushed the timetable back by two months, just long enough for the 12 month building schedule to overrun into what would be summer 2014. The decision was taken by the trust to open in 2015 instead, giving much more time to complete the project.

Ownership of the site transferred to public hands on Tuesday 3 September and was swiftly followed by yet another hearing, this time in the Appeal Court, against the CPO. The court's dismissal of this final appeal by MTCRC was announced on 8 October – ending what had been a legal battle lasting more than two years. The cost of this litigation has not been revealed.

230. One of the many features which helped to earn Grade II* listing for Dreamland's cinema is a pair of statues over the exit doors of the main auditorium. This one was still in situ when recorded in September 2010.

231. A group of enthusiasts was shown around the cinema building by Thanet Council's conservation architect Nick Dermott in 2010.

Throughout the summer tensions between the two sides were running high amid fears by the trust that some of the vintage rides stored on the park site could be sold off by MTCRC – more legal action was threatened by the trust if that happened.

Those fears were realised with news at the beginning of September revealing that a dozen rides had indeed gone from the park – and was confirmed by Jeremy Godden, son of the late Jimmy, who had acquired the cinema building earlier in 2013 from DreamlandLive, the new name for MTCRC, despite the legal process around the compulsory purchase.

He told the Isle of Thanet Gazette the rides had belonged to MTCRC and not the Dreamland Trust. Later, the trust was able to say the items which had been disposed of were intended only as props for the new look park, not operational rides.

With news the Appeal Court had ruled in the trust's favour once more, the trust was quick to name a date when the public could 'take back' the park.

However, a clearly embittered Toby Hunter couldn't resist one final snipe to try and spoil the party. He told the Isle of Thanet Gazette his company would not make any fresh appeals but its claims for compensation 'would cause the council a problem in their statutory budgets for years to come'.

He added: "So far there is no evidence that either Dreamland or TDC have any clue how to build an amusement park, let alone a successful one. You will see they will overspend in the next two years and this will require further borrowing."

The authority dismissed Mr Hunter's claims saying money had been allocated from its reserve funds to cover the cost. The council said it expected to pay only a small sum as the site has no residential rights, despite DreamlandLive's insistence it is worth several million pounds.

The park's gates were thrown open on Saturday 16 November – for the first time in seven years – when some 2,300 people turned up in autumn sunshine to see everything at close quarters. Perhaps inevitably, with the site back in public ownership, the council had made sure new meters were in full operation in Dreamland's car park that day. Still, nobody minded and it was one way of recouping a little of the money it has spent there over the past few years.

On the day, more than 160 people registered to volunteer to help rebuild Dreamland while nearly 80 people potted plants on site to take home, nurture and return with them in 2014 to replant in tribute to the original 1870s pleasure garden while creating a new green space around 'Lord' George Sanger's Grade II listed animal cages.

232. The open day in November 2013 provided an ideal opportunity for people to see inside the park for the first time in seven years. The 1930s buffet, an arcade in more recent times, is no less forlorn than other structures nearby.

233. A surviving part of the Scenic Railway's station area as seen in November 2013. The 2008 fire took out much of the structure immediately behind and to either side but the flames were held back here.

That evening 250 people attended a celebrity fundraising art auction, organised by Fontaine Decorative, in Dreamland's disused seafront amusement arcade. Some £25,000 was raised towards transforming the arcade into a visitor and learning centre. The event was a sell out within a week of announcing ticket sales.

On Saturday 30 November 50 volunteers took part in a Big Clear day to help clear moss, weeds and rubbish from the site. This group included

234. A gratifying sight to see the walkway under the Scenic Railway busy once more as people thronged to view the park in November 2013.

young, middle aged, retired, physically challenged and people with severe learning difficulties. More Big Clear dates are planned during 2014.

The scale of the work to be done before reopening should not be underestimated. The dilapidated, but nonetheless listed, Scenic Railway needs more than £2 million of work to restore it to full working order.

Most of the timber frame will be replaced while new sets of trains are to be specially made.

Nearly as much money again will be needed to fully weatherproof the former ballroom building at the far end of the old cinema block. Built from the original 1860s railway station buildings, it is the oldest structure on the site and requires strengthening and reroofing throughout.

Thanet Council released documents to prospective tenderers for the Scenic Railway engineering and trains contract in December 2013. Several expressions of interest were received and eventually the winning contractors were arriving on site to make inspections by March 2014. The full planning application to rebuild the Scenic was submitted by the Dreamland Trust to Thanet Council in early April 2014.

Later that month the council announced it would be seeking a management company to run the park on a day to day basis through an open procurement process and would outline its plans at a cabinet meeting on Thursday 1 May.

Meanwhile, rides restoration work continues with David Littleboy and Roger Sibley in Wakefield with the intention of exhibiting their progress in the Dreamland amusement arcade visitor and learning

235. Part of the original Sanger built flint boundary wall featuring the now listed animal cages, believed to be the only ones remaining in Britain.

centre after its official opening during the Whitsun weekend on Sunday 25 May 2014.

The former amusement arcade in the cinema building is being transformed by Hemingway Design into an informative, interactive and fun environment evoking the atmosphere of Dreamland and a taste of things to come in 2015.

Run by a team of volunteer greeters and guides the centre will act as a hub describing Dreamland's rich history, the restoration process and future plans supported by a programme of pop-up events and activities in the build up to Dreamland's revival.

With all of this in place and combined with astute marketing and careful stewardship, Dreamland is set to enjoy a revival in its fortunes which will bring more people to Margate and in turn encourage much needed investment and regeneration.

Those involved must not lose sight of the fact that people see the park, first and foremost, as a tourist destination for rides, amusements and fun – not as an outdoor arts attraction appealing mainly to the more affluent middle classes.

But let's leave the last word to Mick Tomlinson, one time advertising manager at Dreamland and in more recent times a Mayor of Margate, who, speaking ahead of the open day in November 2013, told the Thanet Extra newspaper: "People of Margate have stood by the attraction while the sad and sorry saga has made it an easy target and a laughing stock to many.

"This is Margate's big moment, the final chance to get it right at Dreamland and for it to regain its rightful place as one of the top leisure spots in the south.

"Dreamland has been kicked around like a wounded animal for far too long, yet it is still breathing. We want it to roar again."

Jimmy Godden – a footnote

We mentioned previously that Jimmy Godden's son Jeremy had purchased the cinema from MTCRC earlier in 2013 but some may ask what had happened to Jimmy himself in recent years?

By his own admission in 2005 he had decided to take a back seat interest in matters at the park, but was still a minority shareholder after selling to MTCRC. With other leisure and property interests around Kent, he was still actively in business but was diagnosed with stomach cancer in 2010. He died at London's Royal Marsden Hospital in March 2012, aged 66. He is survived by wife Rochelle and adult sons Jeremy and Jordan.

Toby Hunter paid his tribute in the Isle of Thanet Gazette stating: "No matter what many people will say, Jim did a lot for Thanet. He paid taxes and rates, he employed many people over the years. That to my mind, all adds up to something."

Building a new dream